The 5 Steps to Get Your Songs Heard

A Congregational Songwriting Plan

STEPHEN ROBERT CASS

PHOENIX, ARIZONA

SONGS4GOD.NET MEDIA
An imprint of Solid Walnut Music
15620 S. 14th Place
Phoenix, AZ 85048
songs4god.net
Send feedback to feedback@songs4god.net

Printed in the United States of America
10 9 8 7 6 5 4 3 2 1
Library of Congress Cataloging-in-Publication Data
Cass, Stephen Robert
the 5 steps to get your songs heard:
a congregational songwriting plan
by Stephen Robert Cass.
1. Cass, Stephen Robert—Songwriting. 2. Religious

ISBN 979-8-9855371-4-7 (pdf)
ISBN 979-8-9855371-5-4 (epub, ASIN)
ISBN 979-8-9855371-3-0 (pbk)
ISBN 979-8-9855371-2-3 (audio)

Copy and line editing, proofreading:
Pauline Goff and Mandy Williamson of Fresheyesproofreaders.com
Cover design: Songs4God.net Media
Interior layout: Formattedbooks.com
Printing in the Unites States: IngramSpark and Amazon KDP

Significant discounts for bulk print and e-book sales are available by emailing steve@songs4god.net or call (480) 773-3484

CONTENTS

Titles by Stephen Robert Cass

Fishing in Church: How to Be a
Congregational Songwriter
*A blueprint for learning the craft of
congregational songwriting
and getting your songs heard*

The 5 Keys to a Clear Mix: Create YOUR Mix Philosophy
for Christian Artists, Songwriters, and Church Song Mixers

Establishing a Culture of Lead Worshipers:
How to Build a Worship Team
Everyone on the platform is a lead worshiper

The Harmony for Worship Project
Training Voices to Praise the Living God

Worship Songs and the Law
How Churches Stay Legal and Songwriters Get Paid

The Proverbs 27.17 Song Critique Method
The Power of Group Learning to Deliver Songs

For Dr. Chuck Fromm, who believed
that the song always plays a central
role in our relationship with God

INTRODUCTION

DO YOU PROMISE MY SONGS WILL BE HEARD?

I promise this is the simple formula you've been looking for, that you will have the power to write and deliver songs that worship leaders want to sing, and that *you* or *your tribe* will get them into the right hands.

And by the "right hands," I *don't* mean a Nashville song attorney, publisher, or record producer. I mean local churches that are hungry for fresh songs from songwriters driven to deliver them. The "right hands" are worship leaders and pastors that want to download and use your songs from Christian Copyright Licensing International's (CCLI) SongSelect service. These churches are going to report the usage of your song, and you will see the song's popularity blossom.

Any person called by God to write songs can fulfill their dreams by learning the ways of congregational songwriting. Young or old. Experienced or not. Let me show you how to get your songs heard.

The steps to make this possible:

#1. Align your Ministry with Jesus.
　　See his purpose, values, and mission as your own.

#2. Bust the Nashville Myth.
Bust the fantasy that the music industry will save you.

#3. Learn the Craft.
Embrace the unique language of congregations.

#4. Join with Like-minded Songwriters.
Align with fellow travelers in a community.

#5. Get Your Songs Heard.
Sign your songs with a faith-based music publisher so that they are distributed to local churches and the wider world.

GET STARTED TODAY

I write so you'll have a blueprint to begin this journey today. I'm a songwriter with over 120 songs in my catalog—including 70+ songs in my CCLI catalog, and I have discovered over time that CCLI is *the* distributor and a tool of hope along the path of success for the congregational songwriter.

How to open doors for your songs in local churches and how to obliterate physical and perceived roadblocks is what you'll read on the following pages. My experiences as a songwriter and music publisher, along with workshops and sessions I've attended with well-known Christian artists, songwriters, and worship leaders, have prepared me so I can show you how to accelerate *your* growth as a songwriter and remove the roadblocks.

I've been playing on worship teams for over fifty years, been a worship leader for several of those years, and have been a musician playing in over one hundred churches in five states. I am a recording artist and music publisher that has distributed albums to Christian radio stations in fifteen countries, and I will help you break down the walls.

Howard Rachinski, a music minister looking to protect his current church and all churches from lawsuits, founded CCLI in 1984. The organization was originally named Starpraise Ministry at its founding but the name was changed when it was incorporated in 1988. CCLI was born because of the news that F.E.L. Publications sued the Archdiocese of Chicago, seeking $3.1 million in lost revenue due to copyright infringement.

This legal battle between a church and a music publishing company inspired Rachinski to build a business based on two principles: 1) provide legal protection for all churches using copyrighted songs by collecting fees from them and paying the Recording Industry Association of America and publisher members for song uses, and 2) provide a method to pay independent Christian music rights holders for their work.

Rachinski designed the company to do more than issue licenses and collect fees. Their flagship service for churches is SongSelect, a song repository for members, which has an excellent search engine that drills down inquiries by song, author, publisher, topic, and public domain. CCLI features online-transposable chord charts, lead, lyric, and vocal sheets, and mp3 audio previews. They feature integration with third party service planning software such as Planning Center Online, OnSong, and Worship Extreme. CCLI added a Liturgical Calendar search engine in 2019, and have additional cutting-edge video, rehearsal, and streaming licenses to help protect churches and serve worship leaders in the digital age. Find over 100,000 songs at https://songselect.ccli.com.

CCLI also has their own video channel, WorshipFuel, that provides new songs, background stories, interviews, and music tips. These are thoughtful and useful tools to serve music ministers in churches around the world.

Today, CCLI serves over 250,000 churches worldwide.

No, I'm not receiving a commission from them, but I have a specific reason for telling you. I know their value and their system quite well because I am songwriter and worship leader who has used them in the past, and I am a copyright holder and music publisher with them today.

CCLI is a powerful song distribution tool designed specifically for the benefit of the Christian songwriter and the church. CCLI's resources and this plan to get your songs heard stand ready to serve *you* today. By following this plan and taking advantage of the services offered by CCLI, you will be able to publish your music and make your best songs available on SongSelect.

Now, before you think that this is just another way to "level the playing field" so just anybody can upload a song and have it spin among the thousands of songs in their database, let me tell you how it works: CCLI will only accept music publishers who can show they have distribution plans in place. And you will have a convincing plan for them after you read this book.

When you allow CCLI to distribute your songs, they will be available to over 250,000 churches around the world. This five-step blueprint uses their database to concentrate on the primary goal of reaching local communities. Reaching the wider world is a reality, if that is God's plan for you and your songs.

You will use custom *congregational* songwriting tools to sharpen your skills and help the songwriter next to you do the same. Together, you will create a songwriting community designed to nurture like-minded songwriters. The guiding principle is Proverbs 27:17, *"As iron sharpens iron, so one person sharpens another."* Songwriters and those who support them will learn and grow together.

There is a final breakthrough component of the blueprint that takes the songwriting community to the next level: The creation of a faith-based music publishing company aligned with the goals of the songwriting community and individual songwriters.

This grassroots music publishing organization will have the primary goal of seeing the songwriting community flourish in their mission to reach local churches. It will be tasked with all recording activity, execution of legal requirements, handling of all aspects of song administration, and it will control the release of the songs. This organization will have the responsibility of protecting and promoting the reputation of the songwriters and the community and will stand ready to promote it and the best songs from it to the world.

Is it all about making money? Absolutely not. We exist to make Jesus famous. But we will make money along the way to support our efforts.

You don't have to create the songwriting organization or the music publishing company to learn the ways of congregational songwriting. But you need to surround yourself with the people who will.

The following pages will describe each of the *5 steps*.

What's in it for you?

- You will learn a unique set of songwriting skills, never before taught. Anywhere.
- You will become a songwriter sought after by worship leaders and pastors.
- Others will seek you out to co-write worship songs.
- You will be answering God's call to write songs.
- Through your songs, you will take part in God's mission for us all through Jesus Christ: To bring back *shalom* to the world.
- And, finally, you will get your best songs heard.

Are you ready?

The 5 Steps to Get Your Songs Heard

#1

ALIGN YOUR MINISTRY WITH JESUS

His Purpose, Values, and Mission

FISHING IN CHURCH

There's a reason Jesus chose the people who followed him. Some of them were deeply lost in life and needed his lifeboat. But most were just regular people trying to make their way in life. One of the things the core group of disciples had in common, though, was their focus on a particular task: that of catching fish for a living. For those of you who like to fish, what is the first picture that comes to your mind? Actually catching a fish, right? If you have caught a fish, you know what I mean.

Jesus knew what drove that core group. He knew that there was a forever-picture in their minds: A thrill of the chase, an obsession with it, and that this vision was the quarry that sustained their lives. After filling their nets to the brim and proving to them that he was the Master

Provider, he told them they were just getting started. "Don't be afraid; from now on you will fish for people." (Luke 5:1–11)

> *After filling their nets to the brim and proving to them that he was the Master Provider, he told them they were just getting started. "Don't be afraid; from now on you will fish for people." (Luke 5:1—11)*

Even if you don't like to fish, I think you can visualize it. There are those who are so focused on a task that they will do whatever it takes to get the outcome that they are working to achieve. The Father uses this drive within us to draw us close and align us with the Son to complete our mission on Earth. This same yearning keeps you, the songwriter—or you who are called to mix live sound at church or make demos and support Christian music—working for people and for God.

Jesus is calling you and me to fish for people. He recognizes the drive we have because he put it there! So, rather than wallow in the conversation going around in our brains that our songwriting is without guidance and direction, let me offer up this statement. We have a calling. Those of us called by God to write are indeed called by Jesus to use our talent to fish for people.

And where do people gather who seek to know him? They come to homes and multi-purpose school rooms and church buildings and sing together about the God they love. *This* is our mission field. We are called to fish in church.

It's not about "singing to the choir," it's about bringing heartfelt theology in song to people yearning to learn more about *God's* mission to us: His everlasting comfort, love, and salvation. He made that promise clear by giving us his one and only Son, that anyone who might believe in him should have everlasting life. Everlasting life, the fullness of life, the abundant life, begins here and now, according to Jesus in John 10:10, "… *I have come that they may have life and have it to the full.*"

The desire of God the Father and Jesus the Son is for us all to find shalom (completeness, wholeness, health, peace, welfare, tranquility, prosperity, perfectness, fullness, rest, harmony, and the absence of agitation or discord) according to John 14:27. *That's* God's story. That's *our* story to tell in song.

> *"Peace I leave with you; my peace I give you. I do not give to you as the world gives. Do not let your hearts be troubled and do not be afraid."*
> John 14:27

"Peace I leave with you; my peace I give you. I do not give to you as the world gives. Do not let your hearts be troubled and do not be afraid."
John 14:27

Join me and learn the unique pathway of *congregational* songwriting.

SAYING YES

In April 1995, I was sitting on the floor, playing my guitar and crying out to God. "Lord, why did you give me this music gift if I can't seem to write songs?"

It had been twenty-five years since I first learned to play the guitar. I had no trouble writing music, but the lyrics I wrote never seemed to stick. Nothing I wrote seemed genuine or sincere; it was shallow.

As I was praying about it, I heard God's voice loud and clear. I'll never forget the moment of clarity and calmness that came over me. It was as if a veil disappeared from my eyes, and I saw the truth about my existence for the first time. It's hard to explain it any other way.

As I was praying, crying out, and asking God why I couldn't write songs that stick, he told me why. "It's because you haven't been writing about me."

I know it sounds cliché, but I tell you my jaw hit the floor.

I would never say something like "God spoke to me" lightly or give extra strength to the episode just because it sounded cool or important or added credibility to my story.

After a couple of minutes composing myself and thinking of the implications, I reminded God, "But … but you know, God, I have trouble with lyrics." And as my eyes were compelled to look at the Bible, it became crystal clear. "You just stick to the music. My word will inspire the lyrics."

Boom. Case closed. Question and prayer answered. Marching orders given. That's the equivalent of a mic drop, I'd say.

No more confusion.

The songs began to pour from me. At last, here came the songs I was so desperate to write. I had been playing and singing in and out of church since I was twelve, but I didn't have a clue how to write until that day in 1995. God gave me the push that day and I began piling up new songs and gathering the tools to record them.

What began as an inspiration that April day became the creation of Solid Walnut Music, my record label and publishing company. I recorded my first solo album, *Wisdom—Discovery of the Word* in 1998. We produced five CD projects and distributed them to Christian radio stations in fifteen countries. I know we touched lives, and I was hopeful our musical invitation led others toward the fullness of life.

That's one way you can use your time, talents, and treasures to serve God.

FAITH AND ACTION

God was sending me another message at the same time. This was the late 1990s through the early 2000s, when worship music became a popular genre and playing those songs in church was a new thing. If you googled Solid Walnut Music, it was the number one return for the search term "Christian music publisher." These days, I can't even find my company in the search results. Anyway, because of that, my mailbox was flooded with unsolicited demos from songwriters. Many of their cover letters said how desperate they were for someone to give their songs a chance and that I was their last hope.

I continue to be amazed by how many have heard the clarion call to write music for God. Why is it that the spirit of the local church songwriter is stifled? Is the quality of songs an issue? Where is the outlet for them? There are so many songwriters who have been called by God to write, sing, and play. And I know from experience that there is often no other instruction from God other than, *Just write*.

Where does that leave us? If we don't have a blueprint, a plan, or a map, what's next? If we don't *do* something, we'll *stay* in a constant state of angst and frustration.

No matter what we undertake in life or the decisions we make concerning our calling, doubt has a way of creeping in, doesn't it? But just like Mary, the mother of Jesus, there must also be faith. "I am the Lord's servant. May your word to me be fulfilled," the unwed pregnant teenager says in Luke 1:38. It takes the first step of just saying, "Yes!" No matter your fear. *Then let faith fill the space where fear lives in your heart.* Not faith that God will give you fame and the money you want, but faith that you'll take part in advancing God's kingdom by answering his call on your life.

> *It takes the first step of just saying, "Yes!" No matter your fear. Then let faith fill the space where fear lives in your heart.*

Let God guide you to remove fear and insert faith into your heart with the following scriptures. Spend time in prayer with the context of these stories:

Psalm 3:6	Psalm 46:2
Psalm 91:5	Isaiah 41:10
Isaiah 43:1	Matthew 10:31
Matthew 14:27	Mark 5:36
Luke 5:10	Luke 8:50
Romans 8:15	1 John 4:18

Mary would be the first to tell you how confused she was through the childhood and early adult life of Jesus. But she would be quick to tell you how steadfast her faith became through those years. How special an earthly task to care for and nurture *Immanuel* as he grew to be a man, while having faith in *Abba* Father in Heaven.

This desperate call from songwriters to be heard has worked on my heart since that time when I received all those unsolicited demos. I know publishing and recording companies only market sure-money writing, but that's not the only obstacle blocking the road to getting their songs heard. They need to be encouraged to bear fruit. There's just no denying the call from God on thousands of songwriters. I believe God has a plan for them. And I believe God has designed a plan just for you.

> *Allow the worship of your local congregation to reflect songs of how God is moving in your community*

God has a plan for me now to teach the ways of congregational songwriting. Much of my encouragement comes from Dr. Chuck Fromm. Dr. Fromm was a pioneer in modern Christian music and was given the Lifetime Achievement Award by the Gospel Music Association in 1990. He was also the founder of *Worship Leader Magazine* in 1992. I have attended three conventions sponsored by him and *Worship Leader Magazine*. He encouraged me, both personally and in group settings, to begin a songwriting community based on local theology, which is:

> Allow the worship of your local congregation
> to reflect songs of how God is moving in
> your community.

I promised Dr. Fromm that I would keep him updated on my progress, but I am very sad to say I never had an update conversation with him before he passed away in 2020. I am honored to have met him and to have heard his passion for songwriters, the church, and local theology.

My fond memories of his encouragement to me and other worship leaders fuels *my* passion to continue his legacy.

The challenge is, unless we songwriters are a part of a megachurch in the twenty-first century—and one that has already built a songwriting community—we may not have the opportunities to share our work. Yet, great songwriting should be part of every church. The challenge becomes, *How can we make that happen?*

I have created a simple template for education that will help you gain strong technical skills that will produce quality congregational songs. This training doesn't exist anywhere else. I hope you find its value to be equal to the passion I have for sharing it.

I've designed custom tools to shape your congregational songwriting education and get you past the *physical* and *perceived* roadblocks I alluded to in the introduction (and will begin addressing in the next section). I created all of this to nurture local song theology. There's a blueprint in this book for a songwriting organization and a publishing company with the intent to deliver songs to local churches first (the rest of the world later). Ride along with me on this journey, or even better, take all this information and create your own grass roots organization, large or small.

I can envision the future of local worship music, and I accept the challenge God has laid on my heart. I'm saying yes to God for his call to help train you in advanced songwriting techniques and to show you a pathway to get your songs heard. Will you accept *my* challenge and join with me?

THE TASKS AHEAD

Before I introduce my custom songwriting tools, I want to help you see and eliminate the *perceived* roadblocks. The first roadblock is eliminating all personal doubt and desire for personal glory from the call Jesus has for us to fish in church. We need a steady and clear thought pattern as congregational worship songwriters. After agreeing on fishing in church and saying yes, absorb the new paradigm of who you are and what your mission is. This will keep you on track for the prize.

MAKE JESUS FAMOUS

How do we get our songs out there? Clear your mind of preconceived notions and decide to *make Jesus famous*.

- *Know your calling.* All of us called to write songs want to use our gifts for the glory of Jesus. Just saying a blanket "yes" and that you're open to however God wants to use you is not knowing your calling.
  - *Call to Action:* Decide and commit to learn the ways of congregational songwriting. Honor God by learning how to proactively minister to people using your songs in church. *Make Jesus famous.*

- *You can write better songs than anyone.* Decide to rise above the pack and count yourself among the most talented songwriters out there. Today, pledge to write songs that help, encourage and invite people to know Jesus. Decide you'll no longer write just to stroke your own ego but for the sake of others. Pledge to enter the mission field of fishing in church for Jesus.

- ○ *Call to Action:* Feel the power inside as the Holy Spirit inspires you. Believe in yourself like God does. Your call from God to be a songwriter *for* him does not differ from the call he gives to the person called to teach others about his ways. Your gift is to be given away. No matter how your songs sound, dedicate yourself to getting better every day so you can *Make Jesus famous.*

- *There is no such thing as stardom.* No one is waiting to discover you and whisk you into a life of meaning. The music business doesn't work like that anymore. Don't get caught up in hero worship and think that one person's calling is your own. You've got *your* job to do according to the gifts you have been given and the skills you are willing to learn.
  - ○ *Call to Action:* Tell the world and God the only stardom you want is to *make Jesus famous.*

- *Seek education.* Write down specific steps to become a better songwriter. Make a plan to execute those steps. Your songs may be loved and appreciated because your heart is in the right place, but that won't help you create songs that people want to hear again and again. You need more than likes and followers and pats on the back from social media. You need education in creating God songs that others will enjoy.

- ○ *Call to Action:* Take steps to fill your mind with the skill set of a master songwriter so you can be an effective servant for God's people. Find a mentor who understands that the priority is to *make Jesus famous.*

- *You are in charge of writing your plan of success and your next steps.* Understand this: the steps other songwriters are taking may not be the right ones for *your* journey.
  - ○ *Call to Action:* Build an action list to know the right steps for you, depending on where you are in *your* process. Cultivate a network of like-minded people to help you along the path, both mentors and peers. That's where the power of growth lies. You'll stumble along the way, but you'll learn and start to travel the right road. Failure and feedback are the best teachers. The goal is, repeat after me, *"Make Jesus famous!"*

Spend time alone and in conversation with God about how you might be used and fulfilled.

> *Spend time alone and in conversation with God about how you might be used and fulfilled.*

#2
BUST THE NASHVILLE MYTH

Bust the Fantasy that the Music Industry will Save You

"Songwriters have this fantasy that if they can just get their songs in front of the right people, then they'll get a cut or get a contract, and it just doesn't work that way.

Spend energy seeking attention for your songs by raising the level of your songwriting so that you write songs that are worthy of attention.

You can take this to the bank. You can't hide a great song. If you are faithful to sing it [on the internet or in public], it will be heard."
Mike Harland, director of Lifeway Worship

Busting the Nashville myth is not a negative exposé on the music industry, nor some passive-aggressive swipe at the town. It's not judgment on those who live and work there (and God bless the songwriters there listening to his call), nor is it a condemnation of opportunities you can find there. It is a clarification of the opportunities available for worship songwriters in and outside of the industry. And it's a God-view about your calling as a congregational songwriter. Replace the name "Nashville" with any gatekeeping, mental roadblock name you'd give to the music industry.

It starts by taking a realistic look at the second *perceived* roadblock: You think you have to move to a music center to be successful as a worship songwriter. Replace this FOMO (*fear of missing out*) with the transparency of how God views you and your ministry, and how he has created a different path for you than you may think. Next, see the *physical* roadblocks the worship songwriter has with the music industry. Then read a small sample of success that local theology songwriting brings to the world. Lastly, read about the business marketplace built *specifically* for the congregational songwriter.

> *Replace this FOMO with the transparency of how God views you and your ministry, and how he has created a different path for you than you may think.*

THE I-GOTTA-MOVE-SOMEWHERE MYTH— INSTEAD, BLOOM WHERE YOU'RE PLANTED

Writing songs for church carries a different sort of importance vs. any other type of song. Consider blooming where Creator God planted you. There is a reason you are *who* you are and *where* you are. Psalm 139 tells us that *Abba Father* knew you before you were formed in your mother's womb. Woven throughout the Bible are examples of ordinary, imperfect people being used by God in extraordinary ways where they were. He's going to use you, too.

Some people travel to do the work of God. Do that if you're so called. But don't think you have to move to fulfill your calling as a worship songwriter. There are plenty of churches in your hometown. This is where you're needed.

See, God has you where he needs you. Unless you hear the call to move distinctly or just decide to move because you want a change of scenery, consider the Apostle Paul's advice to the Corinthian believers:

"Nevertheless, each person should live as a believer in whatever situation the Lord has assigned to them, just as God has called them…in the situation they were in when God called them." (1 Corinthians 7:17, 24).

Paul was telling them—as well as us today— that wisdom should rule. He recognized that seeking contentment and productivity in our current situation and allowing God to work through us is true wisdom, and how we will best prosper.

Rather than looking around and hoping for something else, look for understanding and insight where you're planted. Rather than thinking that someone in the music industry is going to "discover" you (the industry moved on from that decades ago), use your energy to define your local ministry.

THE PHYSICAL ROADBLOCKS FOR THE WORSHIP SONGWRITER

Gospel Music Association past president and CEO John Styll explains how the Christian music economy is a subset of the mainstream industry. He gives a concise breakdown in the referenced article, saying that popular Christian music needs to look like mainstream music, but on tighter budgets.

> *"Since most [Christian] radio airplay is on non-commercial stations, which pay a fraction of what commercial stations pay in royalties, our songwriters receive far less income than those in other genres."*
>
> John Styll, Gospel Music Association
> past president and CEO

https://www.beliefnet.com/columnists/gospelsoundcheck/2008/10/3-things-you-need-to-know-abou.html

Those mainstream revenues only come after significant exposure and music publisher exploitation. And that's probably a good thing. This underscores why the emphasis has been—and should always be—on the message. The average Christian songwriter often hears about the millionaires made in the music industry, but they may not realize this applies to *very* few Christian music artists.

> *"And the real opportunity in this very difficult season is for gospel music to provide the hope and inspiration our culture so desperately needs."*
>
> John Style, same interview as above

While this is all so mixed up—songs, God, money, and worship—we have a choice: we can arrange it so our lives cross paths with this song economy, or we act at the local song theology level.

Either we're happy with what we accomplish at the local level, or we pursue the business of songwriting and artistry at the business level. Those are our choices. More about the local song level in a minute. First, more myth busting.

WHY APPROACHING THE MAINSTREAM MARKET ISN'T PRODUCTIVE

Building relationships is the preferred method in the music industry, just like it is in any other business. It's not recommended that you send your lyrics and demos to publishing and record company contacts on a cold-call basis, that is unsolicited. Your hard work will not be favorably received. Instead, it will go into a very large bin. Trust me. I have many works inside these large bins somewhere.

There is truth to the adage, "It's who you know," and in the relationships you've established. Songwriters must co-write with successful songwriters who have written hits in the past, so they have a carrot to dangle in front of another publisher to ask for a future deal.

Here are quotes from five solid, real-world music industry authorities about submitting Christian songs, or any songs for that matter, to the mainstream music publishers:

Song coach Robin Fredericks advises:

What are the odds?

"Okay, reality check… Reaching an established artist when you haven't yet built up a track record as a songwriter can be difficult. These artists tend to use songs by writers with a proven

*track record, or they write the songs themselves,
or co-write with the album's producer."*

https://mysongcoach.com/how-do-i-
sell-my-songs/

And hit songwriter Jason Blume agrees and elaborates:

**"For eleven years, I had chased a staff-
writing deal to no avail.** *But once I had a
recording that was likely to earn money, I
had six publishers wining and dining me and
offering me the deal I had hoped for."*

https://bmi.com/news/entry/staff-writing-
what-it-really-means-and-how-to-get-a-deal

*"There's no doubt, it's persistence. Nobody in their
right mind would have thought that I had any
special talent years ago but the special gift that
I think I got was just believing in myself and
refusing to quit. And like I said it took eleven years
for me to sign a staff-writing deal—and five years
after that before I had big hits. And so for me, it
took sixteen years, so the key was persistence."*

https://www.bmi.com/news/entry/ouch-
how-to-cope-with-songwriting-rejection

Mr. Blume has written Grammy-nominated songs
that have sold more than 50 million copies. It took him
sixteen years as a professional songwriter before he started
making any extra money. He's written over 1,000 songs and

received over 10,000 rejections during that time. How does this translate to your chances as a part-time songwriter?

https://promusicmagazine.com/hit-song writer-and-author-jason-blume/

John Thompson, past Creative Director at Capitol Christian Music Group Publishing (formerly EMI CMG Publishing) tells how scarce opportunities are for songwriters:

*"'God's Not Dead (Like a Lion).' Daniel Bashta wrote that song. We heard that song and thought: 'This is just a great song.' Young guy wrote it. We signed that one song and pitched it around and then the Newsboys record it and have a big hit, and now it's rising up in the church and you go, okay, so, there's an example of a guy who came from obscurity with one song. **Those stories are awesome, but they're really, really rare**."*

> *Jason Blume has written over 1,000 songs and received over 10,000 rejections in his first 16 years as a professional songwriter. How does this translate to your chances as a part-time songwriter?*

https://worship.calvin.edu/resources/ resource-library/john-thompson-on-the- christian-music-industry/

It's possible to submit songs as an unknown, as author and songwriter John Braheny shows in the blog post *Getting Heard in a "No Unsolicited Material" World*. But it's not without planning and understanding the market needs of the company.

> ***"Why is it so hard to get through the doors?***
> *To be able to deal with this problem effectively, we need to look at it from the point of view of the publishers, producers, record company A&R representatives or managers who are your most prominent "targets." They have two major concerns: finding great talent/songs in the most time and cost-efficient way possible and protecting themselves from lawsuits."*

https://songwritersresourcenetwork.com/
getting-heard.php

Please hear this message: The music industry is like any other business. If your works can improve their bottom line, then they might listen to you. Take the following messages to heart:

- The major mainstream music companies have Christian music divisions. They exist to help serve, some say exploit, the *performing* Christian artist under contract and Christian music consumer, not discover independent songwriters.

> *"Songwriters have this fantasy that if they can just get their songs in front of the right people,*

then they'll get a cut or get a contract, and it just doesn't work that way.

Spend energy seeking attention for your songs by raising the level of your songwriting so you write songs that are worthy of attention.

> *"Spend energy seeking attention for your songs by raising the level of your songwriting so you write songs that are worthy of attention."*
> *Mike Harland*

You can take this to the bank. You can't hide a great song. If you are faithful to sing it [in your home church or in public], it will be heard. "

Mike Harland,
Director of Lifeway Worship

- Yes, there's room for Christian *artists* to take on the learning journey and perform on larger stages to attract the record industry. But the journey for songwriters is different. You can move to Nashville and pursue getting a job as a staff songwriter, if you'd like. But our primary mission as worship leaders and songwriters is to glorify God in our local communities *first*.
- There's nothing wrong with seeking pay for your work or getting your songs into the right hands where they can become known. There are worship leaders and songwriters who want to make a living with music or are driven by the passion to deal with industry insiders.

LOCAL THEOLOGY SONGWRITING SUCCESS

"… when I say that all theology is local, what that means is, in reality, what is being practiced by the church is not necessarily something that was preached in the seminary. It's something that is practiced in that congregation."
Dr. Chuck Fromm

I attended a songwriting conference for worship leaders in 2013 sponsored by Dr. Chuck Fromm and *Worship Leader Magazine*. I became forever impressed with his sense of just how much power there is in seeking God's influence throughout a community, then writing songs about God's movement. I was so swept up by his level of intensity and emotion about building local songwriting teams in churches that I made it a point to meet him and to attend his workshops so I could interact more closely with him. I shook his hand in hearty agreement about the future of local song theology.

Dr. Fromm isn't the only influence regarding the need for local song theology in today's worship, but his voice has been one of the loudest. I can still hear him saying:

> *"Allow the worship of your local congregation to reflect songs of how God is moving in your community."*

The above is a summary of Dr. Fromm's beliefs on songwriting for the church. It is worth your time to read more about his local theology philosophy. The following quote may better explain the basis of his philosophy:

"To be a worshipping church you need a theological understanding…when I say that all theology is local, what that means is, in reality, what is being practiced by the church is not necessarily something that was preached in the seminary. It's something that is practiced in that congregation. And so local theology is our thoughts about God and His working in us in this community of believers and in our larger communities around us, and ultimately how He has worked with us as a church family."

Dr. Chuck Fromm, Lifetime Achievement Award by the Gospel Music Association in 1990, and founder of *Worship Leader Magazine* in 1992 From *An Analysis of the Need for a Congregational Songwriting Manual for the Evangelical Community*, page 64, by Travis Doucette

https://pdfs.semanticscholar.org/9ce7/59e82 03330c440a460b60bc8439c4b32a322.pdf

You need to know about local song theology, because that is what drives the current era of popular worship songwriting. Here are but a few examples of how local theology songs have changed the course of Christian songwriting history.

WORLDWIDE SUCCESS BEGINS AT HOME

Dave and Dale Garratt of New Zealand founded the record label *Scripture in Song Music* in 1968 and gained international attention with the release of hundreds of songs, both in print and recorded. See https://en.wikipedia.org/wiki/Scripture_in_Song for details.

Chuck Fromm and Calvary Chapel formed an independent record label called *Maranatha! Music* in 1971 to record and distribute songs from the "Jesus Movement." Songs written by these artists were considered unsuitable for "traditional church" and yet introduced lasting church song titles as *"Open Our Eyes"* in 1976 and *"As the Deer"* in 1986.

The Vineyard Church developed Vineyard Music in 1985 and the church wrote its own worship songs. John Wimber of the Vineyard movement founded *Mercy Records* with these creations. This later became Vineyard Worship, who brings us worship leaders, songwriters, and recording artists Brenton Brown, Brian Doerksen, Andy Park, Jeremy Riddle (who had a long association with Bethel Music) and Kevin Prosch. Vineyard Worship has released hundreds of recordings.

In 1983, a small church in Baulkham Hills, New South Wales, outside of Sydney, Australia, began writing their own songs and using them in worship. Hills Christian Life Center, later known as Hillsong Church, started their music ministry intending to write theologically rich songs that reflected how God was moving in their community.

According to Steve McPherson, current manager of Hillsong Publishing and a guitarist in the band in those early years, their label resulted from people asking if they could get recordings of their songs. The church didn't start with any record company plans, but they believed God paved the way for that to happen:

> *"So, it wasn't about selling albums then and it never has been. The priority was writing songs that will inspire the people that God has entrusted us with to worship first—everything else was simply responding to the platform God continued to give to us."*
>
> https://hillsong.com/collected/blog/2014/ 05/the-early-years/#.Ya5-ONDMKUk

Hillsong Publishing started recording and distributing their songs in 1993, and as of 2021 has released over sixty albums (and I'll talk more about Hillsong's publishing model in *Section #5*).

Songwriting communities have sprung to life in large church communities. Bethel, Gateway, Elevation, Jesus Culture, New Life, The Belonging Co., Upper Room and many more. These churches have nurtured songs and songwriters and have recorded and presented their best songs to their faithful people. They have not just recorded them for their own church communities, they have marketed them to the world. And we continue to use them in our churches every week.

Some churches are now reaching out to create larger creative arts communities. Community Christian Church out of Chicago created Community Music, a movement comprised of church planters and artists who work together to equip local and global artists for the mission of Jesus. They sponsored a songwriting conference in 2021 to help conference participants learn about songwriting from professionals, practice co-writing, and create a community of songwriters. A quote from the conference website: "We want to create a worship culture that goes beyond songs and Sundays. God has called us to work out this dream in our local context, across our nation and the world!"

Many communities such as Passion City Church and Elevation Church have their own design on how to create and launch a songwriting and/or artist community to reflect their expression of local song theology. These churches planned to produce records for the mainstream market from their inception.

Many of these church songwriting communities build their own record and publishing companies, although not all of them enter the music business. Instead, they hire out the administration and distribution to the mainstream industry. For instance, Elevation Church signed an administration deal with Essential Records in 2011 and has a distribution deal with Provident Distribution.

Today, there are over fifty independent Christian music record labels.

The point is that Christian music has never needed the music industry to thrive. *However*, with the rise and popularity of local song theology and worship-style music over the last twenty years, the major secular record labels and distributors have created their own Christian music divisions. *(It appears they jumped on the bandwagon because they saw dollar signs. They had ignored Christian music like the plague before then.)*

Some Christian artists or labels that began as independents were absorbed by major entertainment companies. For

Today, there are over fifty independent Christian music record labels.

example, the Provident Label Group, which represents Casting Crowns, One Sonic Society, Vertical Worship, Matt Maher, Matthew West, and many other artists, and which cover myriad labels such as Essential Worship and Reunion Records, is a division of Sony Music Corp. Through this growth period, Christian music has been, and will probably remain, a niche in the pop music market.

An important distinction is that brand awareness and sales drive decisions in the music industry rather than local song theology, spiritual healing and awakening, and the heart of worship. I like to think that although the industry hires people who do care about these things, that's not the business bottom line. Sadly, you can imagine which element wins most often. The substance of worship can only come from the bride of Christ, the church. The responsibility for fishing in church, reaching for the sounds of our grassroots, and knowing our congregations lies with us songwriters and worship leaders.

LOCAL SONG THEOLOGY REVOLUTION

Dr. Tanya Riches spoke at Dr. Chuck Fromm's songwriting conference that I attended in 2013. Dr. Riches has many accomplishments: pastor, songwriter, administrator of Hillsong United, and master's program director at Hillsong College. But perhaps her greatest accomplishment was that as a fifteen-year-old girl attending Hillsong Church she wrote a song for them during a trying time. She related that time of her life to us:

"When I was fifteen, I wrote a song called *Jesus What a Beautiful Name* which ended up in the top ten CCLI songs in Australia and New Zealand. And one thing that I'm very passionate about is that song is connected to a very particular story in our church. It was the first song released after our worship pastor stood down following a moral failure. As a fifteen-year-old, it was quite huge for me to think about because this was the song that encouraged Hillsong Publishing to keep publishing songs … There are sounds that are particular to places and there are moves of God. And we're trying to recreate them. The gospel and worship are universal, but sound is particular. Our job as worship songwriters is to find the sounds of your community … it's really about them. It's about who they are. Worship with the sound from the grassroots."

Hillsong released *Jesus What a Beautiful Name* in 1996 on their fifth live album, *God is in the House*. This was the first album released after Darlene Zschech became Tanya Riches's and Hillsong Church's new worship leader. With the explosion of Darlene's song in 1993, *Shout to the Lord*, and a later 1996 distribution deal with Integrity Music for the US market, Hillsong Music Publishing was soon to become an international phenomenon.

Elevation Church released a song titled *Give Me Faith* in 2013. The songwriting team wrote it in alignment with a sermon series to help their people respond at times when they felt their lives were falling apart (listen to the story at https://www.youtube.com/watch?v=wW8-pzWOspE). It inspired them then, as it inspires us today, to allow God to work through them in spite of their weaknesses, to allow the Holy Spirit to reign in our lives (2 Corinthians 12:9). The song has grown from a local North Carolina church encouragement and grassroots faith story to one among many famous songs from them now sung in churches around the world.

The experiences of Chuck Fromm, Tanya Riches, Steve McPherson, Darlene Zschech, Hillsong Church, and now Elevation Church and many contemporary communities have sparked a revolution in church song worship, and all songwriters should take notice. Their inspiration for music came from their grassroots experiences of church community life.

Yes, there are excellent worship songs available from the national and worldwide markets, and we should sing them. You are an essential instrument of God, and we need to sing your inspired songs, too. Local song theology will thrive because of you as you write about the sounds that come from the roots of your community and because of the movement of the Holy Spirit.

> *You are an essential instrument of God, and we need to sing your inspired songs, too.*

THE NEW MARKET FOR CHRISTIAN SONGS

Another market is especially built for the Christian music songwriter. It's not reserved for big-name worship leaders and full-time songwriters. It's dedicated to *all* congregational and Christian songwriters.

As I mentioned in the *Introduction*, CCLI was founded in 1984. This resource, which has now been available for over 30 years, helps churches honor the songwriters, artists, labels and rights holders who create and own this work by ensuring fair use receives fair compensation. They do this by issuing licenses to help raise funds to pay royalties for copyright holders. CCLI is now serving over 250,000 churches worldwide (https://us.ccli.com/2min/).

> *"With 160,000 member churches in North America alone, CCLI is now the number one source of income for many faith-based publishers and writers."*
> Vince Wilcox, general manager of the
> Discover Worship online song source team
>
> http://blog.discoverworship.com/articles/
> what-is-ccli-and-why-should-it-matter-to-
> my-church

This royalty source is the avenue to pursue for the worship songwriter. I know this to be true, personally. As a publisher member with 70+ song titles at CCLI, I know their system well and have used it to gain exposure for my songs.

It's the perfect solo income source for songwriters who don't take part in the mainstream music industry, or an additional income source for songwriters who plan to gain more notoriety and attract other publishing exploitations.

CCLI is a unique tool for the music industry, designed specifically for the Christian songwriter and churches. It serves the creative artists that want to pursue the business side of music in both the mainstream and independent markets, as the following short story illustrates:

> Ken and Melinda are great friends. They're
> on the same worship team and co-write

songs together. They also co-write with other people. Each of them approaches their songwriting business to their own taste. Ken is the type of person that likes to keep track of all the publishing administration details himself. He's in constant contact with the CCLI intellectual property department to see that his songs are properly registered. Melinda has attracted a publisher in Nashville and is quite happy to let them take care of all publishing administration. Plus, her publisher is pitching songs to other labels and artists.

Many of Ken and Melinda's songs are being used by their church and local churches, and their CCLI revenue has grown significantly over the past couple of years.

For both Ken and Melinda, CCLI is truly a Godsend. Their songs bless the church. Their work is protected and rewarded by CCLI. And they get to keep doing what they love, knowing that their efforts are truly valued.

> *For both Ken and Melinda, CCLI is truly a Godsend. Their songs bless the church. Their work is protected and rewarded by CCLI.*

This is an excerpt from https://us.ccli.com/our-partners/artist-and-songwriters/artistssongwriters-vignette/ Please visit this URL to read the full story.

LOCAL THEOLOGY AND CCLI

It's no coincidence that CCLI was founded at the beginning of this revolution when Hillsong music began their expansion. They were the first company that helped to create a new worldwide market for Christian music.

I encourage you to read the full story of CCLI and their value to churches, how they legally function with the mainstream music industry, and how they pay royalties to songwriters in my book *Fishing in Church* and in my e-book *Worship Songs and the Law: How Churches Stay Legal and Songwriters Get Paid.*

CCLI is easily the best free marketing tool for independent church songwriters and music publishers. They publish their top 100 requested worship songs weekly. The most popular worship songs in the Christian music world are on that list as free promotion on their very popular website, https://ccli.com.

CCLI has become an important tool in this local song theology era and an indispensable player for churches on every continent. The rise of CCLI as a go-between for churches and the music industry paved the way for the next stage of local song theology: the rise of the independent Christian music publisher.

GREATER EXPOSURE FOR OUR SONGS

CCLI has a criterion for allowing songs to have full placement (lyric, lead, chord, hymn sheets and an audio sample) in SongSelect. A song must be reported as used by multiple, specifically ten as of 2021, churches in any one semi-annual reporting period.

They also log calls to their office when churches request song sheets for certain titles. When they receive a minimum of ten calls, they will make the sheets available in SongSelect.

However, any songwriter can request a publisher membership. If accepted, you can register your songs and give CCLI the title, lyrics, authorship, and ownership information, so it appears in their catalog.

Placing the CCLI song number on your lyric sheets lets churches know you are a CCLI member. As churches use your song, suggest they acknowledge the use of your song title and CCLI song number on their periodic reporting to CCLI. Also, have them make a phone call to CCLI to tell them that the church used it.

As of this writing, the only method to know if your songs are used by a particular church is for you to contact them and ask them if they are reporting the use of it to CCLI. Specific church request information is not made available to you in the accounting statements from CCLI.

This is the first step of your partnership with CCLI for digital distribution. Churches report the usage, and your share of royalties will begin.

Your solid and theologically sound songs for the church will pave the way for good discipleship and powerful evangelism. It is an opportunity for us to share the witness of our faith to our local and world church communities.

> *Your solid and theologically sound songs for the church will pave the way for good discipleship and powerful evangelism.*

This gives us a chance to grow our ministry and to strengthen our faith. I personally have a duty to write and deliver the best songs I can for God and his church and don't plan to stop any time soon.

IS IT ALL ABOUT THE MONEY?

We should not limit God if he wishes for us to reap any monetary gain from our songwriting. After all, the worker deserves their wages. However, our motivation is not money. It is spreading the Good News of Jesus Christ. First of all, it is all God's money.

We have a decision to make about serving God with our money. I believe that decision is best approached from the perspective that money is a tool to serve him. Our creativity as songwriters is another. Matthew 6:24 challenges us to recognize that God is our Master, and we can't worship him having an improper attitude toward money. Offering our creativity back to him in worship as a priority over making money from it is evidence that we have the proper perspective. So, the bottom line is that we either see money as a tool for serving God or as a way to satisfy our own greed.

I believe in the principles that Jesus taught about exchange, and how a healthy exchange acknowledges the sovereignty of God over money.

In parable after parable about money, Jesus never talks about how money itself is bad. Rather, he always talks about how the *love* of money over the love of the Father will be our downfall.

He also talked about how easy it will be for our love for money to lure us over the things we ought to do toward the kingdom of God. Luke 18:18–29 tells the story of a rich man who called out to Jesus, and I will loosely paraphrase, "Good Teacher, what must I do to have eternal life?" Jesus says, "No one is good except the Father. You know what to do: No killing, no stealing, no lying, honor your father and mother." And the rich man said, "I already do all of these things." "Well then," Jesus said, "there's only one thing left for you to do: Sell all you have, give it to the poor, and come follow me!" But the rich man walked away sadly, knowing he couldn't do it.

My great takeaway from Jesus's encounter with the rich man is that having an improper attitude toward money will set us up for disappointment and failure. The rich man probably thought he was good enough already to inherit eternal life. But Jesus knew his *heart* and that it was flawed by his *love for money* as a priority over the basic rules of life from God. The man wanted God to justify his selfish hoarding of wealth rather than be willing to use it for God's purposes. God desires that our hearts and minds make this paradigm shift.

Jesus told his disciples that it would be easier for a camel to pass through the eye of a needle than for a rich man to get into Heaven.

He again, so brilliantly, through the communication tool of hyperbole and contrast, shows that money can be our downfall versus seeking the heart of the Father. It will block our hearts as we seek the Father's will for our lives.

In Luke chapter 10, Jesus sends out his disciples. He tells them when they enter someone's house to accept whatever they are offered for food and drink, for the worker is worthy of their wages. Songwriters are worthy of their wages. They, of course, have the right to give away their work, but Jesus supports their efforts to find the balance between the heart of God and a healthy exchange.

And bust the Nashville myth that the music industry is the only way to get your songs heard. Instill the truth that God needs you to bloom where you are planted so your songs will help tell his story on Earth.

I hope you don't think that I got off point. But I believe that we songwriters have internal struggles about this that must be put to rest. Bust the internal-dialogue myth that says the motivation of a healthy exchange of money for your songs is for greed. Turn that idea on its head and let it help you build your songwriting ministry.

And bust the Nashville myth that the music industry is the only way to get your songs heard. Instill the truth that God needs you to bloom where you are planted so your songs will help tell his story on Earth. Learn the ways of congregational songwriting so it can be used as a tool for evangelism and discipleship.

#3

LEARN THE CRAFT

The Unique Language of Congregations

"You can have the greatest band or the world's greatest choir, but if the heart is not engaged in loving and connecting with your Savior—all you have is a great band or great singers—it's just reduced to music."

Renowned worship leader and songwriter Darlene Zschech

There are specific song crafting skills of the genre that best serve our way of expressing thanks to and worship of God. Our people, our worship, and our Savior are each distinct and worthy of skilled analysis to deliver our best return of praise to our Father in Heaven!

You, dear songwriter, are the expert that can deliver theologically strong songs in ordinary, yet poetic, language.

Listed below are the essential heart-soul-mind connections people have as they gather to worship, the songwriter's relationship with God, how what they write compels musicians to lead others in worship, and the tools they need to learn that language:

- The heart of worship
- Vertical connection time
- The power of 1:1 songwriting time with God
- Aligning the power of the song with the heart of worship
- The connection
- The essential tools
  - The Proverbs 27.17 Lyric Formula
  - The Proverbs 27.17 Melody Shape Tool

- The next-level tools
  - Song critique
    - The Proverbs 27.17 Song Critique Method

  - Rewriting
  - Co-writing
    - The 8 Ground Rules for Kingdom Co-writing

THE HEART OF WORSHIP

We had this routine to prepare for worship at Canyon Creek Church in Chandler, AZ when I was there as a guitar player and vocalist around the year 2000. The worship team, whoever was on the schedule for that Sunday, plus any other member who wanted to attend, would meet every Saturday morning at eight o'clock.

The plan was to spend two hours together in prayer, sharing, and book discussions, then two hours for practice for the next morning. We'd meet at seven o'clock on Sunday mornings and practice, do a run-through for the service at nine o'clock, then get together for the service at ten o'clock.

This worked well for us. We had the time to share and cry and ask for guidance, friendship, and prayers from our fellow musician travelers. This gave us the strength to pull together and give heartfelt worship music as a genuine family of Jesus followers.

Johnny, our worship leader, thoughtfully led us through this well-structured and simple discipline which was designed to prepare our hearts to be servant leaders on the platform. Many churches do something similar. One thing Johnny used to tell us was: Any time we didn't feel able to give ourselves fully to the team and to worship—for whatever reason, hey, we're human—to let him know. And if we felt our hearts weren't in the right place to give 110%, maybe we should consider sitting out for a week or two. Or however long it took to get it right.

Johnny, of course, the ever-influential leader, would always come alongside us and ask us how we were doing, pray and cry with us, and ask where we were in our walk with God.

The astonishing part about him was he actually did this himself. There were times he'd take himself out of worship for that reason and his wife, a keyboard player in the band, would fill in as leader. I loved Johnny and his dedicated heart for worship, and his dedication to us.

I was just getting to know him on a more personal level. He and I lived in the same neighborhood, and I'd often pick him up and take him home so his wife could have the car, and we'd have time to talk. I shared with him that it was in my heart to be a worship leader someday.

I gave Johnny a ride one Sunday morning and asked him how he was doing. He said he was having cold sweats.

Other than that, he felt all right. We went through practice and run-through, and everything seemed normal for that morning's worship service. But it would be far from normal. We were singing the song *Be Glorified* when Johnny started having trouble. It started when he began to stumble on the platform. He took a few steps and came toward me and said, "Lead." Then Johnny crumbled where he stood. The doctor afterward said that he was most likely dead before he hit the floor. He had suffered from severe heart disease, unchecked and unmonitored, and that day was his to meet the Lord.

That traumatic event changed me and our little church forever. Johnny left a legacy that would endure. He impacted many with his heartfelt servant leadership and genuine love for each of us. His impressive example of worship and people leadership left its indelible mark on my heart and cemented my love for worship leadership. The power of his approach to the art of worship was in eliminating life distractions from the platform and instead showing pure invitation to the foot of the cross. And he didn't just talk about it, he walked that talk.

This same attitude of the heart for servant leadership in worship musicians is symbiotic with writing songs for worship. The two functions might have different moving parts and responsibilities, but they work together as the same beating heart. They are as important to each other as air is to the lungs. They exist to serve one another as we serve God and his people in church. The crafting of the song deserves our best efforts at not distracting people and

> *The crafting of the song deserves our best efforts for leading others to the foot of the cross of Jesus.*

to be God's vehicle for leading others to the foot of the cross of Jesus.

This type of thinking is best expressed by songwriter and worship leader Matt Redman in his song, *The Heart of Worship*. I attended a songwriting workshop he conducted at *Worship Leader Magazine's* National Worship Leader Conference in 2011, where he told us the story behind the song. Matt's pastor dismissed him and the worship band for a season. The pastor believed the band was only performing and not leading worship with servant hearts. In the song, Matt wrote:

> *I'm coming back to the heart of worship and it's all about you, it's all about you, Jesus. I'm sorry, Lord, for the thing I've made it, 'cause it's all about you, it's all about you, Jesus.*

Learning to be a church musician and worship leader with the heart of a servant is a long and winding road. Songwriters need to feed church musicians and worship leaders with servant-heart songs.

VERTICAL CONNECTION TIME

Servant-heart songs pave the way for people to connect with God. Let's fill our worship services with songs that encourage that connection. The songs will create an atmosphere where folks feel comfortable in crying out to him, where they can commune with him about their daily lives.

> *Servant-heart songs pave the way for people to connect with God.*

As we say "Yes" and "Thank you" to him in these connection moments with God—often called vertical worship—we find nourishment. It's a unique and intimate relationship.

The skillful songwriter helps us sing about this relationship. She makes the promises of the *Greatest Story Ever Told* possible for anyone to experience the nourishment gained when you engage in and find harmony when you connect with God. Lyricists and composers will write songs about how God—who loved us first—continues to pursue us, died for us, and gave us undeserved grace all because he desires that we have fullness of life. God can move us and spark our hearts and minds into action in these connection moments. What an enormous responsibility for the songwriter to convey and what an honor to be his vessel when he succeeds.

There's a unique power in a room dense with songs proclaiming the truth of the possibility of connecting with God. Strong singing in church is a witness to those who are seeking of how the children of God are unified around his story, and of how we respond to the outpouring of his undeserved kindness toward us.

What a testimony it is when visitors come to your church and hear the outpouring of praise! Impressions are usually formed by the music and how the congregation was singing. As songwriters, our job is to make sure they receive this sense of worship at every service.

Helping others to build deep faith is not separate from congregational singing. It is a crucial part of a closer walk with God. People come to church in search of that closer walk.

The congregational songwriter writes about the story of God, skillfully weaving in common emotions and experiences, creating a strong desire in the worshiper to sing his praise.

THE POWER OF 1:1 SONGWRITING TIME WITH GOD

Personal time with God to enhance your relationship and your writing is crucial to foster the *desire* to supply servant-heart songs. This alone makes the worship songwriter unique compared to writers in other genres and critical to finding and developing their heart of worship.

> *Personal time with God to enhance your relationship and your writing is crucial to foster the desire to supply servant-heart songs.*

The real advantage is the power of the passion between you and God, and how you develop your songwriting as your relationship matures. Aligning your heart with him will open a beautiful pipeline of purpose in your Christian walk. It starts as we communicate with God daily. Some of us journal our thoughts as we hear him speak to us, whether it's during our prayer time or through people and situations. This is how we learn to translate the passion in our relationship into our songwriting.

Writing songs becomes an authentic journal of how you wrestle with and adore God (listeners are absolutely attracted to authenticity). It's how we learn to write God's truths and our growth experiences in a way that listeners can relate to and value.

Take an example from King David, who did exactly this. Now we have a book of 150 of his songs, *Psalms*. Here is Psalm 13:

For the director of music. A psalm of David.

> *How long, LORD? Will you forget me forever?*
> *How long will you hide your face from me?*
> *How long must I wrestle with my thoughts*
> *and day after day have sorrow in my heart?*
> *How long will my enemy triumph over me?*
> *Look on me and answer, LORD my God.*
> *Give light to my eyes, or I will sleep in death,*
> *and my enemy will say, "I have overcome him,"*
> *and my foes will rejoice when I fall.*
> *But I trust in your unfailing love;*
> *my heart rejoices in your salvation.*
> *I will sing the LORD's praise,*
> *for he has been good to me.*

Many of David's songs in the book of Psalms contain:

a.   *His questions* or how he wrestles with God or his enemy
b.   How *he pleads* with God to hear him, or he outlines his enemy's failings
c.   He always returns to praise and worship or how God has the solution

Each psalm dwells on one or more of these areas. It's a great formula for a song. But it's born out of his heart of worship which was developed through his relationship with God. This is the sound foundation of a writer who hears the voice of God. It paves the road in the development of good congregational songwriting techniques. It is the cornerstone on which we build our house of song.

Mike Harland, director of Lifeway Worship, said in an interview that the exercise of writing great songs is crucial in developing the skills necessary to write unique and commercial ones:

> *"No such thing as a bad song. They may not be great songs, but the process of sitting down and pouring your heart out to God and writing them is priceless."*
> *Mike Harland*

"We undervalue the process of writing songs, the impact that has on you as the writer. **No such thing as a bad song. They may not be great songs, but the process of sitting down and pouring your heart out to God and writing them is priceless.** Out of the 150 prayers in the collection of the Psalter from King David, how many of those had he written in his lifetime? 10,000? Why don't we hear all of them? Because those songs were for him.

"Question for you: Is it enough for you as a writer if all you do is write songs for God to hear them? If you don't get there as a songwriter, you

> *"If you can get to the point where the process of writing a song for the heart of God is what motivates you, then you might be ready to write a song that motivates others."*
> *Mike Harland*

may not deserve to write one that grabs the attention of other listeners. If you can get to the point where the process of writing a song for the heart of God is what motivates you, then you might be ready to write a song that motivates others."

I hope this last paragraph motivates you to write a thousand songs like it motivates me. What Mr. Harland is describing is what is known as the "x factor." Music publishers aren't looking for great songs, they need *phenomenal* songs. Deeply personal, heartfelt, and well-crafted songs. So does your local church.

ALIGN THE POWER OF THE SONG WITH THE HEART OF WORSHIP

The greatest songs in church act as a catalyst to change mere words and music into passionate carriers of God's truth to our hearts. Songs are how powerful messages and stories are remembered. And these stories are passed on because they speak common truths. The songs give a platform for talented singers and musicians to amplify the power of the passion and open our minds to the movement of the Holy Spirit and the works of God.

My friend and worship leader Johnny was a powerful witness to how we deliver these important truths of God's love by purposeful preparation with focused singers, musicians, and songs. He knew that servant hearts prepared to give 110%, combined with great musical performance, resulted in effective corporate worship. I miss Johnny deeply, but I know he will lead worship for the Lord forever.

We need worship teams to amplify and deliver the powerful wisdom and principles that we songwriters hear in our conversations with God and deliver them into the right hands. We songwriters must focus in order to craft tight lyrics and prosodic music that moves the listener to understand the story of God and cause them to lift their hearts and hands and sing his praise.

Jesus is honored when you align your heart to deliver your best, and you embrace the need to continue to improve on your best. The power that the heart of worship plays in songwriting addresses the *Seek Education* and *Know Your Calling* steps in the *Make Jesus Famous* list from *Section #1: Align Your Ministry*. Dedicate yourself to lifelong learning that will deepen your relationship with God and then be amazed at how that translates to better songwriting. You will discover that both continual learning and spiritual growth are so powerful in corporate worship.

It's not easy to write songs that move hearts, but it's a winning proposition when you combine the effort with the heart of a servant. Conveying your heart of worship in your lyric is the key differentiator between successful songs in church and any other song.

> *"I've written a thousand songs. I may release one or two of them a year if they're any good."*
> *Keith Getty*

As Grammy Award-winning songwriter Keith Getty has said, "I've written a thousand songs. I may release one or two of them a year if they're any good." Let your efforts as a songwriter be aligned with the heart of Jesus as he deepens your relationship with the Father. Then experience the free and permanent gift of the Holy Spirit that gives you strength to fish in church, not for your own reward, but as a dedicated agent of Jesus.

THE CONNECTION

"I think that the biggest failure of songwriting textbooks is not so much on technique, but more on the function of songs and in the community. ***The biggest lack of understanding is the connection between theology and worship and music."***

Dr. Chuck Fromm, Lifetime Achievement Award by the Gospel Music Association in 1990, and founder of *Worship Leader Magazine* in 1992 Taken from *An Analysis of the Need for a Congregational Songwriting Manual for the Evangelical Community,* page 64, by Travis Doucette

https://pdfs.semanticscholar.org/9ce7/59 e8203330c440a460b60bc8439c4b32a322.pdf (bold text is mine)

That is exactly why I wrote this book and the companion book *Fishing in Church*. It's the connection between theology and worship and music. But beyond the concept of *why*, I need you, the songwriter, to see I'm not trying to reinvent the wheel on good and basic song education. There is literally a ton of written material on writing songs. What I *am* doing is inventing the wheel of the *connection* between theology and worship and music. As far as I know, that has never been done.

So, I want to move next to *how* they are connected. There *is* specific songcraft education relating to congregational songwriting that I'll show. But first, try to visualize that the bridge, that is, the connection, between great songwriting skills and local song theology as a *marriage. Like a marriage, the best result is when the two become one.*

The difference between our genre and any other is how applicable storytelling and relational language skills *connect* with the heart of worship. This doesn't happen in any other genre. Sure, there is a heart connection in great lyric writing of any type, but not the heart connection with the power of the Holy Spirit and God's ability to move among his people. And in our songs, content is literally King. Our lyrics are paramount and convey the story of Jesus. They relay theological truths that the world is hungry to hear in a way that is not possible by other means.

> *The difference between our genre and any other is how applicable storytelling and relational language skills connect with the heart of worship.*

Add the unique skill set of the *higher calling* and *discipleship* (concepts which are elaborated in *Fishing in Church*) in the connection, and we have a truly exclusive skill set for the congregational songwriter.

WRITING SONGS FOR YOUR AUDIENCE

In many ways, the congregational songwriting genre is like others, where all the great and rudimentary crafting tools apply. We use similar writing techniques, like creating pictures using similes, such as, "like the fragrance after the rain," or the use of anaphora, the repetition of a word or phrase at the beginning of successive phrases, such as "all my heart, all my soul, all my strength." But notably absent are the "cute" trick phrases, such as the consonance, "nobility has the ability for reciprocity" or wordplay such as, "Central Perk." We use many of the same great literary devices, but not so they draw attention to themselves.

Knowing about:

- The *connection*

    and to

- *Steer clear of lyric devices that draw attention to themselves*

shines a brighter light on discerning what works in congregational songwriting. What does work? To always remember you need to:

- *Write for your audience*

    and that

- *Songs are stories*

Imagine you're driving. The car is your songwriting vehicle. The road you're on is the *connection*. Like the tires of the car, your song creation is rolling along and clutching the road, every inch forward promises a new adventure. With both hands on the steering wheel, you see the reminders: On your left hand is written "write for your audience" and on your right hand "songs are stories." Warning signs ahead alert you to "steer clear of cute lyric tricks."

This is the mental picture of you traveling the road of congregational songwriting. You know that the connection between you and the road, the information that shows that your songwriting genre is quite special, is crucial for staying alive! You also know that to successfully stay on the road, you must make constant adjustments, remembering that you write for your particular audience and that songs are stories. And the obvious part of the picture is that you want to live through the experience, to keep the connection between you and the road, so you're going to obey the warning signs and steer clear of cute lyric tricks.

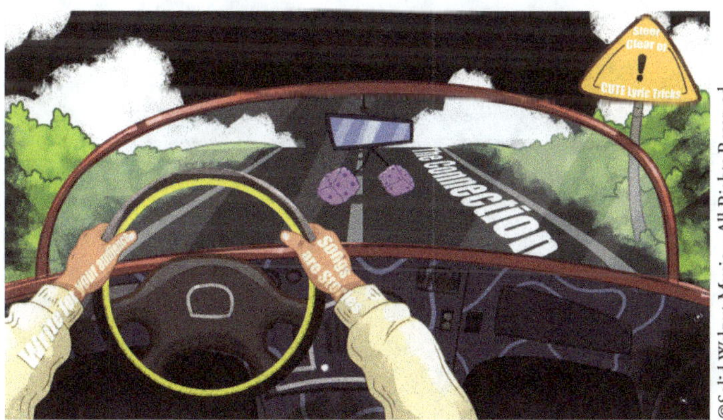

The Congregational Songwriting Car

This scene could apply to any songwriting genre. The *connection*, the ideals and principles native to your audience, and the *warning signs*, the signposts that help you stay true to those mores, will look different, of course. But *write for your audience* and *songs are stories* are universal. So that's the point: Our fuel to create congregational songs is *remarkably* unique. We—and I mean our audience—are laser-focused on our connection, meaning our theology, worship, and mores. Like no other genre!

We write songs for church congregations so people can sing in one spirit of worship to God Almighty. The striving church songwriter focuses on the audience; the audience figuratively and tacitly writes the descriptors for the connection and the warning signs. There is no question among songwriters or communicators of any stripe that finding and writing to and for your audience is the recipe for success. But our audience is different because we are unified in our adoration of the Father. Now *that's* a recipe for success.

THE ESSENTIAL TOOLS

"In advertising, you have this small window to say the most you can. That's what songwriting is. The difference is that you get to put leaves on the trees and color 'em in."

Garth Brooks

THE PROVERBS 27.17 LYRIC FORMULA

How can you be sure the song you write is a strong one? How can you guarantee it will stick in the memory of your listener? How can you get the listener to concentrate on the idea you're laying down?

The answer to all three questions: Realize the song is not about you, it's about your listener.

There is nothing more frustrating than having a great idea but not knowing how to hone it and get it in a form that communicates your story. You know your audience, so craft your stories for that audience. The best way to get started is to latch on to a proven lyric writing system. This will help you go after that unique lyric that defines commercial songs. Don't tell yourself that what you write isn't worthy. Just write and write and write. Remember that King David probably wrote 10,000 psalms, but only landed 150 on his greatest hits.

Here's a preview of my formula for writing a great lyric. I call it *The Proverbs 27.17 Lyric Formula*. Proverbs 27:17 says, "as iron sharpens iron, so one person sharpens another." You or your co-writers should purposely invite others to critique the song later and help you make it better. Great writing is a team sport.

Below is the outline of the formula. I go into rich detail of it in each section in my book *Fishing in Church*.

You'll find an infographic of this at https://songs4god. net/the-proverbs-27-17-lyric-formula. There is a link on that page to download a PDF version you can print out and place on the wall or keep in a songwriting binder.

DESIGN

The **overall architecture** of a great song has these key elements:

The Power of One Idea

- o Other lyrical ideas that you have for the song should support the main idea of it. Every line of the lyric should support the main action of the One Idea. All supporting lines are thoughts surrounding the One Idea.

Prosody Begins with the Lyric

- Prosody defines the rhythm, stress, and intonation of speech. The definition of prosody—whether in poetry, speech, reading, or music—implies that the creation communicates best when there's a lyrical synergy among all parts. That synergy among all parts begins with the construction of the lyric around the One Idea.

A Story (No Story, No Song)

- No matter what type of song, it's *always* about a story, or a part of a story. It might not be a story song, but there's a story that shaped—or is shaping—the main idea kernel.

PREPARE

Prepare by gathering the building blocks for your lyric. Have sessions to mine the most important words and phrases associated with the One Idea. Gather ideas and phrases from:

- Object writing sessions
- The Bible
- Your walk with Jesus

- Your experiences
- Sermons, blogs, word cloud, etc.
- Object writing to capture the relative senses and feelings
  - Your inspiration library (public and private)

Use the resources above and write all things sensory on the topic.

- How does it make you feel? Can you describe any other emotions that come from the One Idea? Are there any smells or tastes involved? Are there any elements of touch? Or sounds? Or color?

Word cloud (writing and connecting related words and phrases on a single page)

- Explore and connect associated thoughts, words, and emotions

BUILD

Build the framework with your blocks by developing these **essential elements:**

Create a Memorable Title

- The title is the product. It conveys the central thought and is the nerve center of your story. It advertises the central idea and emotion.

Design the Payoff

- ○ *The payoff* is described as the line or a phrase in the song that gives the listener ultimate clarity for your message. It's often your One Idea, your main idea.

Build the Schema

- ○ The schema is setting the logical story order for a lyric. The listener needs this so they don't pause and think (and stop listening). They just follow your lead. It's giving them a heads up about the five Ws (who, what, when, where, and why) so you can lay the rest of the lyric on this framework.

Develop the Plot

- ○ Develop *how* you'll tell the story. This goes hand in hand with …

Progress to the Payoff

- ○ Continue to build listener expectations in the plot development toward the payoff.

Choose a Song Form

- ○ Sometimes done consciously, sometimes a secondary concern. More important than the form is the communication of the One Idea and the story you develop. But keeping lyric form in mind can be a great tool/template to develop your schema and plot and tell your story.

TOOLS

Craft your song for the benefit of your listener using tools such as:

Exposition, Conflict, and Resolution

- This tool is a nice and neat template to build your story or song parts around. You expose the scene or your singer's point of view or surroundings and tell of the singer's problem or situation. Then you resolve or move the scene forward with action or solve the problem.

Storyboarding

- This is a productive way to develop the plot by taking each line of your lyric, or basic story idea, then writing that on a 3x5 card. Also note on the card what's happening with your song character, any of the five senses involved, or describe any scene.

Picture and Caption

- To develop visuals and sensory perception for the listener, create snapshot images of the scene in the mind's eye of the singer, from the perspective of the singer. How is the story developing? What's going on with their perception? How can the singer best relate the story to the listener? Now write down the scene.

A Strong Start

- It's good to give the listener a strong word picture or message about the main idea within the first line or two. But more than just strong writing, tell the listener about the schema.

Rhyme

- Using rhyme in writing helps us to remember stories. But the fact is writing rhyme for the sake of rhyme only works for limericks. Not songwriting (unless that's your thing). Rhyming is a memory tool, not a tool to look cute. It's such a powerful tool. It's so powerful that it's easy to seem trite.

Word Economy

- Christian artist and songwriter Morgan Cryar calls word economy "word PSI (word pressure per square inch)". Give more meaning in fewer words. Pack a punch with as few words as possible.

> *Pack a punch with as few words as possible.*

Literary Devices

- o Literary devices help the reader analyze and understand your words. There are many from which to choose, but steer clear of those that draw attention to themselves and distract the listener and detract from the main idea of the song. Here's a solid resource: https://literarydevices.net/

Contrast

- o Use contrast so the listener keeps interest in your song. This works as well for the lyric as it does the music. For example, if your verse uses short words and phrases, use longer phrases in the chorus. The possibilities are many. Take a look at https://lyricworkroom.com/song-anatomy-101/how-contrast-makes-any-song-more-compelling/

The Proverbs 27.17 Lyric Formula Infographic

THE PROVERBS 27.17 MELODY SHAPE TOOL

A memorable melody is the secret sauce of telling your story. If you have a great melody and sharply focused lyric that causes people to sing, you've got something.

> *A memorable melody is the secret sauce of telling your story. If you have a great melody and sharply focused lyric that causes people to sing, you've got something.*

When congregations sing well, that's an indicator that the melodies are sticky. A great worship service is, in part, memorable when people look forward to coming again and again to sing about their faith.

As you create and tweak the melody, be conscious of the:

- Range—the note range and singability
- Shape—the visual structure
- Repetition—how certain elements repeat
- Rhythm—the prosody of the melody with the spoken cadence of the lyric. Does the melody follow and complement the natural speech? Also, does the underlying beat of the music complement or compete with the melody?

I created *The Proverbs 27.17 Melody Shape Tool* to help keep an eye on all these aspects of a worship song. It's a visual aid for those who perform song critiques. You can make comments on the range, shape, repetition, rhythm (and *The Cry*, the top note or set of notes).

Here's an example from the most popular song of the twentieth century (according to the 2001 joint survey by the National Endowment for the Arts and the Recording Industry Association of America). *The "Cry"*, or top note, for *Over the Rainbow* isn't shown here. It's in the song's verse. But some consider the octave jump to start the song *The "Cry."*

OVER THE RAINBOW

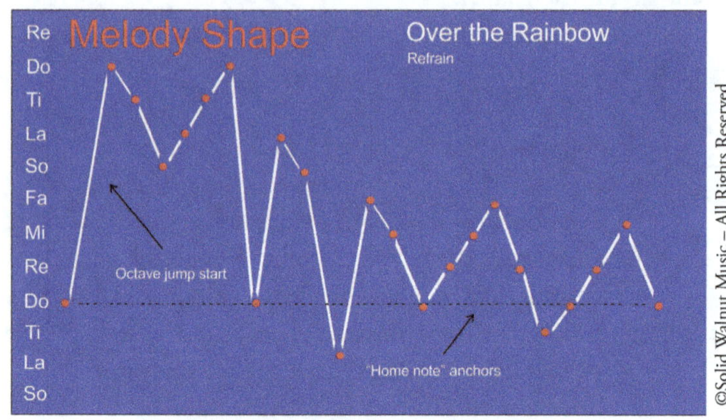

***Over the Rainbow* using The Proverbs 27.17 Melody Shape Tool**

Range—10 notes. Singable, but more of a pleasure to hear a good singer perform it.

Shape—The octave and other jumps and easy-moving melody create a beautiful, easy-flowing staircase. The shape is visually pleasant and shows tight note intervals following the jumps.

Repetition—Three nice jumps to great effect. The first octave jump sets up the melody with a strong start. The second and third are six notes and answer the first. This entire refrain is a beautiful set of fall-away patterns.

Rhythm—Good. The words are sung conversationally. No awkward syllable stresses. The backbeat of the song is simple, instrumental moves complement the melody.

Using *The Proverbs 27.17 Melody Shape Tool*, you can see that the melody shape of this song is phenomenal. The multiple-repeatable patterns make this a memorable treasure, and a pleasure to our ears.

THE NEXT-LEVEL TOOLS

"Songwriters write songs, but they really belong to the listener."

Jimmy Buffett

There are three skills that the serious songwriter embraces to take their writing beyond casual:

- The art of the song critique
- Rewriting
- Co-writing

By "casual" I mean that the writer doesn't care to improve beyond the musings of the heart. Your willingness to master and use the tools above will set you apart from casual. Each tool is as important as acclimating to the 10,000-foot level before you continue the climb and is just as rewarding. Technically, rewriting is the primary product of a healthy song critique. A seasoned songwriter shapes and reshapes a song so it becomes as focused as it possibly could be.

Further, the tools impact the birthing of great songs. When you co-write, a song takes on a different dimension.

> *Technically, rewriting is the primary product of a healthy song critique.*

Multiple viewpoints create the song on a focused idea. In this same spirit, multiple people involved in the critique of a song can ensure it is fully analyzed. A critique team, for example, will look to see that the lines are focused on the One Idea and can encourage rewriting any lines and words that do not support it.

So, these song crafting parts are interdependent and mutually beneficial—they are solo and team skills that expertly shape songs. By mastering your skills on these tools, you will become an important cog on any songwriting team and a part of a healthy and growing local theology songwriting organization.

When you embrace and master these three skills, your talents and results as a songwriter will be amplified. Not only that, the success of your songwriting organization, which I talk about in the next chapter, depends on it. Mastering these skills is a stepping-stone into the larger world for you as an advanced songwriter—because they are part of the DNA of modern worship music.

THE ART OF THE SONG CRITIQUE

One of the best feedback tools is learning the art of the critique. It is equally important to learn how to give a critique as it is to receive one. Embracing this art is invaluable for rewriting your best work. Seeking feedback from a trusted source and using feedback are the best ways to improve as a writer, and both are instrumental in learning to spot writing inconsistencies. When your songs are critiqued, you don't have to make all the changes suggested. But you need to listen to the critique *without taking offense*—and only incorporate the changes that make sense to you … as you *realize* the suggestions improve the song.

No doubt about it. Our songs are our "babies," and we think: "You're gonna attack my baby?!" When I give a critique I say, "This is just my two cents. Take whatever suggestions ring true to your heart and leave the rest." I want them to know my evaluation of the song is clinical.

I will also be sure to include praise for what the song does best, in my opinion.

Learn to take suggestions and ask for clarifications. In the end, you'll need a "thicker skin" to mold and craft songs that will stand out from the crowd. This is all part of maturing in the art.

TYPES OF CRITIQUING

Do you remember the old saying: You have to learn to crawl before you can learn to walk? Here, learning to crawl means to learn how song critique works so you know how to receive it and learn from it. You should learn how to combine the best from "give" and "take," for they are inseparable. As babies, our legs and motor skills strengthened as we grew. We learned to stand and then to walk—but we fell a lot in the effort to get on our feet.

In the songwriting arena, we get to our feet by getting feedback on our songs. Receiving feedback runs the entire gamut of emotion, from getting praise from family and friends to hearing suggestions from a critic you *perceive* as tearing you apart as a person. However, getting only pats on the back or being unprepared to discern constructive criticism won't show you how to get on your feet and become a better writer.

One of the best articles I've seen on waking our minds up to this is *Ten Things Your Mother Won't Tell You About Your Songwriting* at https://songs4god.net/ten-things-your-mother-wont-tell-you-about-your-songwriting/.

Some writers have figured out how to receive critique, but not give it. They only pass on encouragement when critiquing, but do not offer specific suggestions for improvements. Such encouragement from experienced writers is valuable, but not necessarily constructive. You need feedback *designed* to help you get on your feet, take your song to the finish line, and *show* you *how* to be a better writer.

If your goal is to become a dedicated congregational songwriter, "cut to the chase" and take on serious critique. Learn from the critique. Focus the learning and become a better writer so you can cross that finish line.

> *If your goal is to become a dedicated congregational songwriter, "cut to the chase" and take on serious critique.*

You need constant feedback dedicated to your growth. Top-level critique will speed up your learning curve in remarkable fashion to help you create a top-tier song.

But where do you find this information? Is there a single source of information designed to critique and build congregational worship songs?

Yes.

It's right here in the following paragraphs. My intention is to help you learn the art of song critique and harness the power it will have on your writing.

> *Learn how to take data and turn that into information, information into knowledge, and knowledge into wisdom.*
>
> Neil deGrasse Tyson

To do this, I'll show you how to take extensive data from a song questionnaire and turn that into information. Each person on a critique team rate and give comment for each area (this makes the critique team really dig into the lyric and the music). The completed questionnaire is then given to the songwriter so they can take the information and improve the song. Or ignore it. Hey, it's their song, they get to choose.

PURPOSEFUL CRITIQUING USING THE PROVERBS 27.17 SONG CRITIQUE METHOD

This is a next-level tool. It's a method to assess your songs and to learn crafting through *purposeful* critiquing. The design takes advantage of group learning. It is focused on writing for congregations to accelerate the learning curve and sharpen core writing skills. The model includes evaluating:

- Lyric writing
- Melody creation
- The prosody of the music and
- The viability for songs in the church environment

You'll evaluate your own songs and the creations of other dedicated songwriters. I base this evaluation and critique form on five critical song areas:

- Substance
- Structure
- Melody
- Prosody
- Viability

The following is only a sample of the questions and evaluations that you will drill down in the five critical areas:

Substance

- Intended use
- The power of One Idea
- The story aspect
- The central emotion
- Scriptural accuracy

Structure

- Strong start criteria
- Song form
- Rhyme
- Literary devices
- Sound repetition
- Memorable title
- Build to a payoff
- Word economy

Melody

- Singability
- The range
- The repetition
- The rhythm with the spoken cadence
- The shape (visual structure)
- The "Cry"

Prosody

- First, do the lyric and melody belong together?
- Is the lyric conversational?
- Is the intended emotion conveyed throughout?
- Does the song make you want to sing it?

Viability

- Can the chorus stand alone?
- Which ideas or images need expansion?
- Is the song easy to sing by the untrained masses?
- Would you characterize the song as congregational? What are your comments?
- Are the lyrics from the heart?
- Does the song have commercial value?

The definition of congregational songwriting is found in the full version of *The Proverbs 27.17 Song Critique Method* questionnaire which is written in my book *Fishing in Church*. It seeks extensive information about the song by asking follow-up questions to those in this list. You will find questions and criteria there not in the above list.

The PDF version of *The Proverbs 27.17 Song Critique Method* infographic can be found at https://songs4god.net/wp-content/uploads/2022/02/Proverbs-27.17-Song-Critique-Method-Infographic.pdf

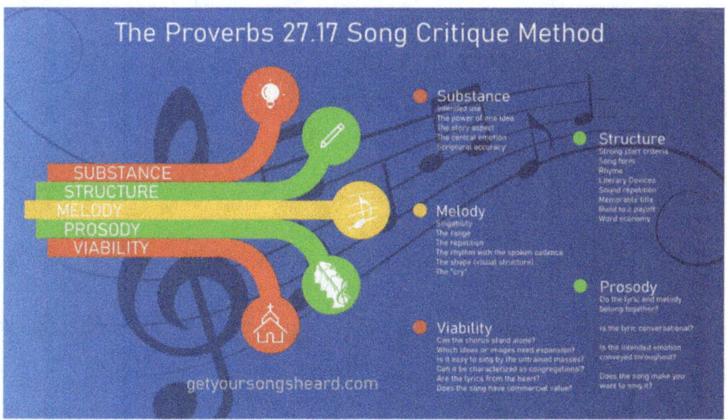

The Proverbs 27.17 Song Critique Method infographic

REWRITING

"The Holy Spirit is the Ultimate Songwriter, but he chooses to flow through us to express himself. The more adept we are at crafting His messages, the clearer they become."
John Chisum, songwriter, former publishing executive for Integrity Music and VP of Publishing for Star Song Media

Imagine if I were to stand up and sing, "Holy, holy, holy are you Lord God Almighty. You reach into my heart and my life and teach me your ways of love and life. Spirit, be with me and cleanse me. Cleanse me. You're so sweet to me, and I love you forever, forever, forever. Hallelujah, hallelujah. Spirit, stay with me now and always, amen, amen, amen," as a reflection of an extraordinarily personal and powerful time of prayer and devotion.

Then imagine that afterward I were to mine some nuggets from that prayer of praise to create a singable song:

> Holy God Almighty
> Fill my heart and life with your ways
> Spirit, cleanse and be with me
> Stay with me all of my days
> Hallelujah, Hallelujah!
> Holy God Almighty
> © 2020 Steve Cass

… then I'd be sharing my inspiration in a way that others could now join in and sing.

I'd never tell you that the crafted version of my prayer was better than when I got up to sing that original free-form prayer. But like the above quote from John Chisum, enjoy becoming adept at crafting a clear message for others to hear so they can join in and sing if they are so moved. And they will be moved when you distill this powerful inspiration.

There may be times we want to use that sort of free-form, in-the-moment spiritual connection time in a church service. But there are also definite times, probably the majority of the time, for people to sing in one loud voice to their King. There's a need to express both styles.

REWRITING A LYRIC FOR THE LISTENER

> *Rewriting is writing. Rewrite the lyric until it no longer needs explanation.*

Rewriting *is* writing. Rewrite the lyric until it no longer needs explanation.

A songwriting teacher asked a student to read their lyric and then explain it to him. When the student was through explaining, the teacher said, "Ok. Be prepared to include that side note with every publication of the song." The teacher was saying, "Why didn't you say what you meant in the first place?"

From the start, craft the song as you or your songwriting team intend the message to be. When you receive critiques, take to heart the messages of how others hear your song. Don't let the defensive attitude of, "HEY, I was trying to get XYZ across!" prevent you from writing what you mean to say.

Don't let your angst meter peg so high that it gets in the way of reading and understanding how your song was received.

After all, they're the listener.

Here are three reasons for rewriting:

- *To build a solid song that congregations will enjoy singing with confidence*
  - You'll learn what congregations expect to hear when they want to sing along in church.

- *For continuing education to sharpen your song crafting skills*
  - As in any good growth strategy, you'll continue to challenge yourself to reach the next desired level.

- *To become an expert in crafting congregational songs*
  - You can pass along what you've learned. You'll become a go-to cowriter because of your communication skills and knowledge base.

We write with the passion to communicate cohesive, clear, focused, powerfully touching, and scripturally sound lyrics for congregations to pray together in song.

That's why we rewrite until the lyric needs no explanation … so we say *exactly* what we intend it to say. Write so the lyric is unambiguous and on point.

I get it. We all want to write and say things uniquely. And a great lyric improvement for a song *is* to add the flair of the poet. But your lines won't hold up with the listener unless you present a clear message.

SHARE AND BUILD ON PUBLIC DOMAIN SONGS

In another method of rewriting, Chris Tomlin and Louis Giglio used a public domain song and made a new copyrighted version. Here's more on how they made a new work from an amazing old hymn.

The new title is *Amazing Grace (My Chains are Gone)*. Chris sang the original hymn much like it is known, but made a few changes (music, lyrics, and music arrangement are the basis for the copyright). They added a bridge.

Though a title itself is not copyrightable, it's still the banner for the new creation. He changed the banner to acknowledge the original work created by John Newton in 1772 and announce the new one by adding the parenthetical *My Chains are Gone*, the hook of the new song.

Now, the underlying new work of words and music is copyrighted. His record company copyrighted the sound recording. Both are now available so mechanical licenses can be issued.

Worship leader Tommy Walker has done this for several public domain hymns. One notable new creation is a version of the popular hymn *To God Be the Glory*. He added a bridge section and copyrighted the song in 2005.

You can do this, too, if you wish.

The list of criteria to determine whether a song is in the public domain is a little long. Generally, as of 2022, any song written prior to 1926 will be in the public domain and therefore available for anyone to perform, rewrite, or record. The use of any of them is free of any royalties due to the owners of the song.

Check out https://www.pdinfo.com.

CO-WRITING

> *A co-written song takes the very best of the people in the room; it's a product of all, not input from one writer to help another complete their individual song.*

Our primary goal is to serve our local communities with song. So, serve the song first. Our reason for writing with each other is to serve the other writer with the best of our abilities, so our efforts are doubled or tripled. A co-written song takes the very best of the people in the room; it's a product of all, not input from one writer to help another complete their individual song. We have a common goal to serve our God and his people with our creations.

Just as iron sharpens iron, we need each other to create the best songs possible. There will be times when you'll write songs solo, then there will be times you'll collaborate with another person or two … or three.

You will find that co-writing is totally different from your solo writing experience, and that it can sharpen your solo writing skills because of the special discipline required to create a song with others. You'll find a new type of writing from the solo writing experience.

The bottom line is that all of your efforts together are to serve the song, to write the best song possible. The attitude among all is that you're together for your best efforts on that day. You will have a bad day and your co-writers might have to take up the slack, but you will also have constructive days when you're the one called upon to lead the others in the writing room. You all need to agree to that reality.

You become a team, and decisions are driven from your unified purpose. When you co-write, you are all-in. All co-writers receive equal credit for the song, no matter the contribution. You agree that you will keep working on the song until all co-writers are satisfied with the product, and you all agree to share in any costs to demo the song.

Most important to relationships, you agree you will not take the song to any other co-writers without the knowledge of the current co-writers.

There is a code of honor between songwriters. Like all good relationships, boundaries and rules should exist. You can honor this code together with a simple written agreement.

As with all contracts, seek legal advice. Or not, on this one. Just keep it simple.

8 GROUND RULES FOR KINGDOM CO-WRITING

1. Prepare
    a. Have a conversation or an email exchange in advance with your co-writers about any song-type or style expectations. For example: Is it a singable, congregational-style song or other? Specify the type. Is it a song for a special occasion such as a communion, Easter or Christmas, or call to worship?
    b. Decide if you will bring ideas to the table, or if you will brainstorm ideas at your first meeting.
    c. Have the discussion about what success looks like. Who is the target audience? What are the expectations for the song?

d. Unless it's already inked in the co-writing contract, talk about publishing administration for the song. Is the goal of the song to—someday—record and release it? Have you designated any one of you to have power of attorney, meaning all co-writers agree beforehand that the goal of the song is to be recorded, and one of you has the power to give the legal permission to give permission for all of you to say it's ok for a record company to record?

2. Know Your Strengths and Weaknesses
   a. You might be great at melodies but challenged when it comes to writing lyrics. Know going into your collaboration what is needed to bolster the other for success. Get to know the other songwriters beforehand to determine their strengths and weaknesses for a better match in the writing room.

3. Be on Time
   a. Show your commitment to success by always being on time for appointments.
   b. Be clear with all communication.
   c. Be prompt and consistent with all things.

4. Find a Way to Say Yes
   a. "No" should not be used carelessly or callously. As a matter of fact, it's good to say no when establishing boundaries. You will find that during writing sessions, saying yes is more constructive than saying no.

Make your "no" known in your co-writing agreement or in your initial conversations. In the session, temper your reactions with things like, "I'd rather ..." or "Can we concentrate on ..."

b. Allow your time together co-writing to be fruitful toward the common goal of producing a memorable song. Find a way to agree—or at least be gracious—and let it be known that you will consider any possibility from your co-writers.

c. You can let your individual assessments of your writing sessions determine the constructive conversations for your next session.

5. Be Patient
   a. Let the better part of your valor be discretion. We're all broken people trying to get our point across. Some of us do that with more grace than others.
   b. Allow people to fail and to say the wrong things. Give them a chance to come around to great mutual conclusions.

6. Encourage
   a. Some of you will have more writing experience than others. You'll often find another writer can do a certain thing better than you, or they know more than you. Listen to the stories from each other. Encourage each other to succeed, no matter how long you've been writing.

b. Our most creative moments come when we know we have the freedom to fail. Encourage team creativity by fostering an environment of support and mutual respect.

7. Be Honorable
    a. Show your co-writers that you intend to produce an awesome, co-written song, not a solo effort with their input. If you discover that your co-writer is a slower thinker than you, be gracious. Your team is set to succeed together.
    b. When hard times and disagreements come, remember your commitment to each other to see this project through to the end. If you decide to put it on the shelf for a time, so be it. Experience any failures and successes together.

8. Be the Co-writer Everyone Wants to Be With
    a. No one will show everyone they're the perfect co-writer. Each of us will fall down at one of these points from time to time. But the mark of experience and maturity is when writers recognize their mistakes in a co-writing relationship and make amends.
    b. The Golden Rule 2.0 applies here pretty well, I think. "If you want others to want to be with you, you should want to be with them." Then show up.

If you strive to pay attention to these points, writers will call on you again and again to help produce winning songs.

NEXT STEPS

Study these topics and tools of the craft of congregational songwriting:

- The heart of worship
- The power of 1:1 songwriting time with God
- The connection between theology and worship and songwriting
- The Proverbs 27.17 Lyric Formula
- The Proverbs 27.17 Melody Shape Tool
- The Proverbs 27.17 Song Critique Method (and rewriting a lyric for the listener)
- The 8 Ground Rules for Kingdom Co-writing
- Share and build on public domain songs

These are the *essentials*. They establish the baseline for the congregational songwriting style. Each of these areas deserves to be studied fully in order to mine the richness of communion that songs bring to our relationship with God and each other. Songs that are rich in sound theology help us to know God in a deeper way and they compel us to stay in touch with the Holy Spirit.

God built us to tell stories. That's how we learned to communicate, and that's why songs touch us so deeply. Songs are stories. We have passed down our way of life and our experiences through them. All songs are inspired by stories, even if the song itself isn't a story song. Songwriters have the distinct honor and privilege of creating and delivering messages about the *Greatest Story Ever Told.*

The "songs are stories" topic and each of these essential topics and tools have been developed more fully in my book *Fishing in Church.*

#4
JOIN WITH LIKE-MINDED SONGWRITERS

Align with Fellow Travelers in Community

"But seek first his kingdom and his righteousness,
and all these things will be given to you as well."
Jesus, telling his listeners the priority
of God in Matthew 6:33

The next step in the journey toward getting your songs heard is to join with a community of songwriters, administrators, and technical people who support your vision. But make no mistake, you can take this step by joining forces with one or two other writers and begin your own community. You don't need to build a sizable community, but you should continue reading to see how this can be done and then modify it for your needs.

Jesus said, *"Where two or three are gathered in my name, I am there in their midst."*

The local song theology solution, what I call The *Proverbs 27.17 Small-Church Revolution,* happens in two parts:

- Inviting songwriters called by God to seek congregational songwriting education, and
- Building a symbiotic worship songwriting organization.

This blueprint will work on a larger scale, but it is designed to inspire you, the creative ones to learn the ways of congregational songwriting and to get your songs heard in your local community. You can be sure that even if your local church isn't listening to your songs, there will be plenty of others who will. *"Seek first the kingdom of God and his righteousness, and all these things will be given to you as well."*

THE SMALL-CHURCH LOCAL SONG THEOLOGY SOLUTION

My blueprint is a small-church local theology song solution for all songwriters, musicians, sound engineers, record producers, and song administrators of any size church.

What do I mean by "small church"? I briefly mentioned this in *Section #1: Align Your Ministry with Jesus:*

> "The challenge is, unless we songwriters are a part of a megachurch in the twenty-first century—and one that's built a songwriting community—we may not have the opportunities to share our work. Yet great songwriting should be part of every church. How can we make that happen?"

Why may we not have the opportunities? Unless your church designs a songwriting community from its inception, it is not likely to begin one until it is a large church, if at all. That's because it takes dedicated personnel and resources to create or sustain this particular ministry … especially with end goals for the songs. Unfortunately, but understandably, most churches don't have that sort of time or bandwidth.

Often when churches try to begin a songwriting community, the effort is led by the worship leader whose primary responsibility is creating a culture of worship in the church. Yet, even if the worship leader is in favor of this additional ministry, and it is fully supported by the pastor and church leadership, it is unlikely to be completed effectively unless it receives the attention and resources it deserves. I would love to support my worship leader if they tried to begin a songwriting community. But I know from experience that a full-time worship leader's time is filled with song administration and creating a culture of worship on the team and in the church, as well as fulfilling other staff responsibilities.

How do we make great songwriting a part of every church? We invite the songwriters from within churches and create a songwriting organization *separate* from any church, separate from the obvious important ministries needed to sustain houses of worship.

How do we make great songwriting a part of every church? We invite the songwriters from within churches and create a songwriting organization separate from any church.

The songwriters of the organization write songs from the experiences of their churches. The songwriting organization feeds our churches with songs.

If we design songwriting communities with the purpose of producing and promoting quality congregational songs, local song theology will thrive in the smaller- and medium-size churches. If we intentionally nurture talented writers for the sake of the community, churches will thrive because of it.

PARTNERSHIP

The small-church local theology song solution is a plan for worship leaders and the songwriting organization to be the new gatekeepers for songs in local churches. Worship leaders are looking for fresh songs to introduce to their congregations, and it's my contention that they should not bear the burden of finding them alone. They are already busy. So, while they select songs for their worship services, the songwriting organization will make new songs available to them.

Partnership.

A partnership with worship leaders or other church leaders energizes this songwriting organization that is composed of one or more songwriters dedicated to the heart of worship and serving all churches in a local community.

How does this partnership happen? Relationship building. Writers need good relationships with their local worship leader, but I'm referring to the relationship between the organization and worship leaders.

Many small churches are without a worship leader. Pastors would be thrilled to know there is an organization that cares about delivering quality songs to them.

If a worship leader is also a songwriter, they might introduce some of their songs to their church. But it also means they may be open to finding songs that communicate the spirit of their congregation. Most would be very open to finding excellent songs from writers in their community, songs that align with the pastor's message and the heart of the church. And so, it is important that the songwriting community looks to nurture and encourage songwriters to deliver songs that are meaningful to their congregations.

Worship leaders would be impressed with a dedicated congregational songwriting organization that wants to help their cause. A worship leader myself, I often feel like I'm alone in the world and sometimes in over my head. Sometimes it seems there is no one to help. I imagine other worship leaders feel the same way from time to time. This is where the songwriting organization can step in and let them know they exist to help. It will energize worship leaders when they understand how serious the songwriting organization is in their mission. Worship leaders need to find fresh and pertinent songs, and we can serve them.

> *Churches and worship leaders need a sympathetic songwriting organization that has a process in place to provide new songs.*

Worship leaders are also managing other aspects of church and worship team dynamics. They certainly do not need more on their plates. Churches and worship leaders need a sympathetic songwriting organization that has a process in place to provide new songs: one that understands and addresses concerns church leaders have about the quality and availability of songs that meet the needs of the congregation, and one that anticipates concerns others may have about the organization. For example:

- The heart of worship within the organization
  - They may wonder: "Is that the true nature of the organization, or are there other agendas? How will they stay on point to serve my church?"

- A process exists to execute the organization's song service
- A published roadmap of what worship leaders can expect from the organization, namely:
  - Technical leadership and details, and to see plans of action in place. How does the organization:
    - select songs?
    - make songs available for worship leaders?
    - develop songwriters?
    - manage song publishing administration?
    - produce demos or other recording projects?

When we manage these questions, and advertise that we do, worship leaders will see how valuable the songwriting organization can be. Some worship leaders may not be ready to use the organization, but they need to be impressed by *our* complete readiness and the presentation of undeniable quality songs. Hopefully, they will see how this can take the pressure off of them.

REACHING OUT TO SONGWRITERS

The partnership plan:

- Worship songwriters dedicated to learning congregational songwriting techniques
- An organization dedicated to local song theology that supports them
- Churches and worship leaders willing to partner with the organization

It all begins with reaching out to songwriters. Songwriters in their churches may or may not have any opportunity to contribute songs to their church. But by joining the local songwriting organization, they will find that they can have a voice in their community and an opportunity to share where before they had no avenue. The number one job of the songwriting community is to get their songs heard by their local churches.

It is the organization that takes the lead to communicate the availability of the songs with worship and church leaders. The songwriter potentially will not have to do any heavy promotional work or communication for the organization. The songwriting organization becomes the voice and champion for the songwriters.

I encourage songwriters to ask about starting a songwriting community in their church, but I often hear that there is excitement to build a community, but there are no clear, strong end goals in mind. Sometimes, because of other commitments, a lack of support, or unforeseen delays, plans don't come to fruition. Other priorities in the church often take precedence. The biggest concern and angst of church songwriting community members are to have plans in place, but those plans do not produce results. They often question how to get their songs to the worship leader or to anyone that will listen to them. The heart is there, but the result is often an "up-in-the-air" challenge of distribution.

> *I want to encourage songwriters in churches to see the value of a more organized and dedicated song community—outside of any church—to reach your worship leader and church leadership.*

I want to encourage songwriters in churches to see the value of a more organized and dedicated song community—outside of any church—to reach your worship leader and church leadership.

THE INVITATION

I am excited to invite you to join or begin a *Proverbs 27.17 Small-Church Revolution* songwriting community based on local song theology.

If you are an experienced songwriter at *any* level and:

- Struggle with confidence and are not sure if you will pursue a solution
- Think you will never be a strong enough writer to compete
- Have no musical skills but a deep desire to learn
- Not sure where to find song ideas
- Can start songs but don't know how to finish them
- Are afraid to show your songs for fear of rejection
- Fear you will never become the songwriter you were designed to be

- Are overwhelmed with where to begin
- Have anxiety to get it done because you know this is the best way to express thanks to God
- Are stuck in a loop, creating the same chords and melodies in your songs
- Are looking for a solution to reignite passion for your songwriting
- Had success in the past, but want to take your craft to a higher level
- Are a worship leader who writes songs, but so far, the songs are not getting favorable responses
- Are frustrated and have analysis paralysis, and God designed you to write great songs. But you need direction
- Know it's not about the money, it's about the message. You want to get paid for your work, but spreading songs of hope and inspiration is more important
- Feel like giving up sometimes, because you are afraid to approach your worship leader
- Feel that your lack of experience or training will be apparent to your worship leader
- You need guidance, but don't want to take up the worship leader's time
  - The worship leader often shares the same perceptions about the writer and wonders if they have the capacity to shepherd them.

- Feel that the only avenue you have is to approach the mainstream market, and you feel you'll never be up to that standard

... then this songwriting community is for you. I invite you to take part and grow while you help others do the same.

As I talked about in *Section #2: Bust the Nashville Myth*, the songwriting organization and the individual songwriter can flourish in part by using the best marketing tool ever created for the Christian songwriter: CCLI. CCLI became an important tool of the new local song theology era during the rise of Hillsong. The song ministry of Hillsong Church was purpose-driven: First, deliver new worship songs for their local community, then actively pursue worldwide distribution. CCLI was a large part of their success from the standpoint of song visibility to other churches. This same song visibility from them will help propel your songwriting organization in this next stage of the *small-church revolution.*

As Dr. Fromm personally encouraged me to begin a local theology songwriting organization, I want to personally encourage you. Maybe you don't want to start an organization. Maybe you're comfortable getting together with another writer or two first. But let me show you how this type of influence will spread in the future.

SHOUT TO THE LORD

There's a reason a song called *Shout to the Lord,* which came from the early Hillsong Church, has remained one of the most popular worship songs in the world for thirty years. They began with and maintained a rich, focused basis of local song theology. Hillsong Church made concrete decisions in those early days to define their local music ministry *(know your calling)* and on how to publish their music for their ministry *(you are in charge of writing your plan of success and next steps)*. Yes, it is a skillful, life-changing song written by their worship leader, Darlene Zschech, but the world wouldn't know about that great song without the commitment from Hillsong Publishing to follow God where he was leading them in getting their songs out to their community, and for them to forge ahead with emboldened hearts on their next steps to get that song and others out to the world.

> *The world wouldn't know about that great song Shout to the Lord without the commitment from Hillsong Publishing to follow God where he was leading them in getting their songs out to their community, and for them to forge ahead with emboldened hearts on their next steps to get that song and others out to the world.*

IT'S NOT ABOUT THE SONGWRITING ORGANIZATION

This grass roots idea of a local song theology solution—a small-church songwriting revolution—isn't to just make records and create hit songs. Sure, that would be nice if it happens, but that is not the focus. The songwriting organization has no obligation or concerns other than to deliver songs full of skill and spiritual truths to the people of God in their local communities. Its mantra:

As iron sharpens iron, so one person sharpens another

Proverbs 27:17

The power of this servant organization lies with how local songwriters sharpen each other. I designed the custom songwriting tools mentioned in the previous section with this mantra in mind. Teams can have greater impact and add more value when they realize they are stronger together with the single goal of honoring God and their churches with their songs. It's not about the songwriting organization; it's about the mission to make disciples for Christ.

> *This new songwriting community, dedicated to construction of congregational music, will be the songwriter's advocate and their voice.*

Individual worship songwriters need an advocate who will be their go-between. The organization will be their champion, supporter, and promoter to the churches and community at large. This new songwriting community, dedicated to construction of congregational music, will be their voice.

God willing, this will bring worship songwriters and artists of a town or a city together like nothing that has ever been done. We can bring hope to those who are called to write songs for God so they can bring hope to others.

THE SONGWRITING COMMUNITY BLUEPRINT

Remember, the organization is separate from any church. But you do need a commitment-driven vision caster in leadership, 100 percent dedicated to the success of the songwriters and the community.

No matter the size or the vision, *the mission* for the organization remains:

- *Help each other become the champion songwriters for their congregations.*
  - Sharpen each other with continual worship songwriting activities: speakers, mentors, lyric and melody crafting exercises, song review boards, workshops on worship songwriting philosophy, co-writing, critiquing, advanced songwriting techniques, and learning how to share the songs with their worship leaders (The organization should take the responsibility of contacting worship leaders; however, everyone should always foster a great relationship with their local worship leader.)

The two main methods:

- *The writers or the group identify their strongest songs. They create simple demos and lead sheets in preparation to share the songs.*
  - This could be as simple as sharing a few songs between churches to blossoming into a full-blown record label. It just depends which way group leadership wants to go.
- *The group or the writers register their songs with CCLI to prepare for multiple church use.*
  - Song administration is key to generating success.
  - No matter the size of your organization, this is a must, because CCLI SongSelect makes the songs available for local, regional, and national church audiences.

- ○ The organization generates revenue because of this association.
  - ▪ To bolster songwriter confidence
  - ▪ To begin funding future organizational causes

To help keep the focus on the mission and the methods, start with a small leadership team of maybe three people. Having an odd number on the leadership team will help you stay on track and provide for majority voting. Manage this list of top-level activities and functions:

- A regular leadership feedback meeting
- Meetings about time commitments and administration goal setting
- Songwriting meeting agenda topics
  - ○ Worship songwriting philosophy curriculum
    - ▪ Any of the essentials mentioned in *Section #3*
      - ◆ The heart of worship
      - ◆ The power of 1:1 songwriting time with God
      - ◆ The connection between theology and worship and songwriting
      - ◆ Proverbs 27.17 Lyric Formula
      - ◆ Proverbs 27.17 Melody Shape Tool
      - ◆ Proverbs 27.17 Song Critique Method (and rewriting a lyric for the listener)
      - ◆ The 8 Ground Rules for Kingdom Co-writing
      - ◆ Share and build on public domain songs
  - ○ Lyric and melody crafting exercises
  - ○ Guest speakers or other activity

- o Critiquing forum
- o Open mic
- o Breakout writing sessions
- o Song promotion forum
  - Songs ready for promotion to churches
  - Songs selected for the next recording project

Again, if you're new and have no connections to get songs recorded, align with the right people. Start small. Act as if you will grow to the level of releasing recordings into the market. Organization objectives and tasks:

> *If you're new and have no connections to get songs recorded, align with the right people. Start small. Act as if you will to grow to the level of releasing recordings into the market.*

- Record basic or full-band demos
- Create lyric sheets and chord charts
  - o Work toward these outcomes. Don't do it all yourself. Surround yourself with people who know how.
- Song marketing
- Organizational marketing
- Treasury
- Membership dues
- Cost of doing business reimbursements
- Royalty distribution (more specifics in the next chapter)
- Song administration (more information coming)
- Songwriter technical education (ditto)

SONG CRITIQUE FORUM

The lifeblood of this songwriting organization is the song critique forum. I cannot stress enough the importance of creating an environment where songwriters can learn and grow to be better in their craft. Build such a one where they will learn the value of co-writing and collaborative relationships with other professionals. At the very minimum, an effective song critique forum will allow each writer to develop songwriting techniques and experience personal growth. They will also witness the growth of their peers and the organization as they journey together and celebrate together when their best songs are released. A song critique forum will become a regular activity and a part of the group DNA. It's a must for writer and songwriting community advancement. It is designed intentionally so you, your writing partners, and the community excel at a rapid pace. Group learning inspires each member—each one challenges the other to grow. Iron sharpens iron.

A song critique forum will become a regular activity and a part of the group DNA. It's a must for writer and songwriting community advancement.

Mastery of all the custom and next-level tools will amplify your talents and results and fuel the engine of the songwriting community and your future publishing company.

The basic formula for *The Proverbs 27.17 Song Critique Method* is in the previous chapter. You will find an in-depth view of the art of the song critique in my book *Fishing in Church*.

PREPARE THE DEMOS

First up, decide on how you want to record your simple demos. You can make a simple demo or if you really believe the song has promise, it might warrant a full-band demo. Regardless, decide at the outset if you will record demos in-house or seek outside help at another studio.

Remember, start small and work toward this outcome.

An important part of organizing the structure of the songwriting organization is to create a selection committee to agree on which songs will be recorded, then create digital or physical albums or EPs (whether CD, vinyl or mp3 audio, or mp4 video). Or you could even create Spotify singles and publish these regularly for any type of distribution.

Engage one or two people in the group to create lead sheets and chord charts to distribute with the recordings. To ensure consistent chart production, it would be better to have a single point of contact for this function.

Now is a great time to cultivate relationships with the audio engineers and chord chart gurus in your life.

> *Now is a great time to cultivate relationships with the audio engineers and chord chart gurus in your life.*

Next up, you should create a plan to make your works available to worship leaders and pastors. You could do an email blast announcing your worship song and making physical or digital packages of your demos and chord charts available on a website. There are many ways to approach the marketing function created by people smarter than me. But one interesting way would be to create an online blog or occasional email newsletter and receive sign-ups. This will create an email listing for future publication of your newsletter or blog. Each newsletter and blog would have helpful articles and information plus an offer to purchase the products.

Look for creative minds, maybe outside the songwriting organization itself, to help with a social media campaign and find what works for your group.

Consider hiring out playlist marketing and private marketing consultation to spread your work to worship leaders and the right audiences for your works.

No matter which marketing approach the organization agrees on, the key ingredient is to create and cultivate relationships.

PREPARE TO MARKET THE DEMOS

Song administration, and specifically songs registered with CCLI, is the preparation for success! The next order of business for the songwriting organization is to register your songs with CCLI to prepare for multiple church use. This is more than placing songs in a marketplace. Joining CCLI is a critical part of the plan to help individual songwriters and the organization make their songs available to local churches first, then to the wider world.

I have to mention here that I don't work for CCLI, even though I keep mentioning it. I simply believe in the reason it was created, its mission, and how we can use it to accomplish our own goals. Explore their website, www.ccli. com, and I think you'll agree.

Registering your songs with CCLI is an absolute must for three reasons:

- You are advertising the need for CCLI protection for churches.
- You are encouraging the church to adhere to the law and to help pay you for your work. For an in-depth report on church song usage and legal obligations, see my special report PDF *Worship Songs and the Law: How Churches Stay Legal and Songwriters Get Paid* and my book *Fishing in Church*. (if you need copies of these books, please visit https://getyoursongsheard.com for bundled offerings and https://amazon.com/author/stephenrobertcass for individual books).
- By providing the CCLI song registration number, the church can report the usage of the song.
  - CCLI bases their decision on whether to make lead, lyric, chord charts and audio samples available on SongSelect by how many churches report the use of the song. They also recommend that you send them an email with the church information if you receive requests for your songs. They will document these requests.
  - When your songs reach CCLI coverage criteria, churches can download the CCLI version of the chord, lead, and lyric sheets.
  - Your song products will be available in SongSelect. Their chord charts and lyric sheets are adjustable by song key before you print them. This is perfect for the churches that request your songs, and your songs will be available for download by over 250,000 churches around the world.

HOW TO REGISTER A SONG WITH CCLI

The organization will apply for CCLI publisher membership and assign agreed-upon songs to the organization's CCLI song catalog. If a songwriter already has a publisher membership with CCLI and they write a song for the organization, they can elect to have those songs assigned to the organization's song catalog. Or they can negotiate song ownership percentages between the CCLI catalog of the organization and the songwriter's CCLI catalog.

The bottom line is that everything is negotiable. The organization will represent new songwriters or songwriters that have never had a CCLI publishing account, while contributing writers with established accounts should negotiate.

Becoming a publisher member with CCLI is a process. Send your request via their contact page on their website. After their internal review and deliberation of your request to become a publisher member you will be notified of their decision. One of the criteria they use in their deliberation is whether you or any associated songwriters are already meeting their minimum requirement for songs available in SongSelect, that is, five or more churches requesting your song. If you do, your request for membership will most likely be granted.

Even if you do not meet the minimum requirement, tell them that you or your writers intend to write songs specifically for congregations and wish to establish the relationship with them today.

You can register the lyrics of your songs, even if you don't meet the minimum requirements for SongSelect representation. These lyrics will become a part of CCLI's searchable database. Churches may still select your lyrics and you can receive print copy credits on the songs.

Register your songs with CCLI as the copyright owner or as a publisher who has the right to administer the works of others. No matter if you register them for yourself as an individual songwriter/publisher or register them for a group of writers as a publishing company, the song registration system at CCLI is the same online tool. You will receive individual song numbers that you will publish with the song information so churches can report the song usage. What you learn when you become a publisher member:

- You will have access to online software and a physical form option to register songs with CCLI.
- There's an online portal for members to view all agreements, access your account, and payout information.
- The Intellectual Property section of the portal allows you to view all the songs in your catalog as well as upload new ones.
- You'll receive a complete accounting report, semiannually, for each reporting territory around the world that includes the number of credits your songs received for the use of:
- SongSelect lyric, chord, lead, and hymn sheets, as well as print, record, translation, and streaming credits.

PREPARATION FOR INCOME SOURCES

Income from digital royalty sources should be offered as continuing education for us all. Digital royalties and mechanical reproduction licensing are changing in the US because of the Music Modernization

Act of 2018. https://en.wikipedia.org/wiki/Music_
Modernization_Act.

It's a fluid situation that demands attention.

Frequently update writers in your songwriting group on how royalties work. Talk about upcoming changes in the copyright laws that might affect them. Make it a point to have presentations and discussions with all members about royalty income sources.

> *Make it a point to have presentations and discussions with all members about royalty income sources.*

The bottom line is that all forms of royalties and fees in the music business should be a part of the member communication plan. All income distribution is the prime responsibility of the organization.

Here is the larger view of possible income streams:

- Organization membership dues
- CCLI royalties—goes to the song rights holder of record
- Performance Rights Organization (PRO) writer income—goes straight to each writer (in the US)
- PRO publisher income—goes straight to each writer, if they signed up with the PRO as a publisher *or* goes straight to the songwriting organization if the writer signs a publishing contract with them (in the US)
- Physical and digital sales of recordings
- Song exploitation income
  - Print and digital sales of sheet music
    - Individual sheet music and folios (song collections or multiple pages)

- ○ Mechanical reproduction licenses
  - ▪ Others who want to record your song pay a mechanical reproduction fee, song track licensing

- ○ Synchronization licenses for film and TV
  - ▪ Broadcasters pay for the use of the underlying work

- ○ Grand Rights
  - ▪ When your music is used on the drama stage

- ○ Foreign Royalties
  - ▪ Royalties and usage fees collected outside your country

- ○ Unforeseen collections
  - ▪ Income from exploitation not on this list, or from technology yet known

These are the largest and most likely sources of income. CCLI income from the full local theology song distribution effort is the most probable in the beginning. In any case, you should concentrate on CCLI income and administration, more than the other areas. But in the long term, be prepared for the other income sources.

Mold your ideas for your songwriting organization around these basic income streams to determine how much attention and effort you will give each source of income.

I can't emphasize enough that it's not about the money from CCLI; the value is in the song distribution through them.

There is more information about income sources in Section #5: Get Your Songs Heard. There are even more details on income sources, royalties, and building a faith-based publishing company in Fishing in Church.

GETTING OFF THE GROUND WITH MEMBERSHIP

Membership in your songwriting organization is to encourage ownership, accountability, and commitment for accomplishing the tasks at hand. Design membership criteria that will be the gateway that motivates participation in setting and accomplishing the goals of the organization.

To do this, I recommend that you develop the criteria based on three levels of membership:

- Associate Member
  - A writer or musician interested in the goals of the group. Until a writer understands your vision and the responsibilities of all members, I'd bring them on as an 'associate' member.

- Writer Member
  - A writer or musician who has signed a contractual agreement with the organization committing to the goals (more about what might be in the contract in *Section #5: Get Your Songs Heard*).

- Support Member
  - A person who offers support to the organization, who has expressed interest in becoming a member, but is not under contract.

Membership is an interesting conversation all by itself. You will arrange and rearrange this over time to find the right fit for what you're doing. The idea is to organize and exactly define each level of membership along with its responsibilities.

Membership can support your recording and song administration expenditures.

Dues? That's your call. But consider that a person is more apt to be committed to what they invest in. You could start with $5 per month or $50 per year for an Associate Member, $10 per month or $100 per year for a Writer Member, and $5–50 per month for a Support Member. There should be a dedicated fund in place to cover demo and song preparation expenses, pay for top-quality guest speakers, and investment into song catalog management. You can prepare any sort of scheme to raise funds.

Dues isn't a profit idea. It's an incentive to sustain the goals.

Dues isn't a profit idea. It's an incentive to sustain the goals.

WHAT TO EXPECT

Don't let your lack of knowledge and experience scare you at this point. I encourage you to keep the community simple so you can focus on the music, serving local congregations, and get your songs heard. But the songwriting community you have created will take you and like-minded people even further as you learn and grow together. It will amplify your efforts as a congregational songwriter.

Section #5: Get Your Songs Heard will dive into leadership of your songwriting community and provide a music publishing and record company building overview. Share this section of the book with other like-minded songwriters who might have the organizational bug.

NEXT STEPS

Remember, you don't have to create the songwriting organization to learn the craft of congregational songwriting, but surround yourself with people who would consider it. I'd be thrilled to give you an honest assessment and my opinion of your situation. Contact me at the information in the *About the Author* section of the book.

#5

GET YOUR SONGS HEARD

Sign your Songs with a Faith-based Music Publisher and Distribute Your Songs to Local Communities and the Wider World

To do the work of others is slavery. To do the work of God is true liberation.

Anonymous

THE GOAL OF THE MUSIC PUBLISHING ORGANIZATION

This grassroots music publishing organization will have the primary goal of helping the songwriting community flourish in their mission to reach local churches. It will oversee all recording activity, legal compliance, and administration. It will also control the release of the songs. Further, it will have the responsibility of protecting the reputation of the songwriting community and the songwriters, and it will stand ready to promote your best songs to the wider world. All in God's will and timing.

You, the songwriter, and you, the person supporting songwriting, have invested your heart, your time, and your brain power to learn how you can make this songwriting dream a reality. Joining with like-minded people in a songwriting community is the first crucial step to getting your songs into hungry churches.

This next step is also crucial because it amplifies the results of the songwriting community. Recording, developing, and delivering song demos might be the responsibility of someone in the songwriting community, but *how* all that actually gets done might also be accomplished by someone in your new publishing company.

> *The songwriting community and the publishing company must be symbiotic. They need to function with the same mission, getting songs to local churches.*

The songwriting community and the publishing company must be symbiotic. They need to function with the same mission, getting songs to local churches. Some of the tasks of the publishing company will be:

- Recording and producing demos
- Creating lead and lyric sheets
- Marketing digital music and lead/lyric sheets
- CCLI/PRO song administration
- Songwriter publishing agreements
- Songwriter management (something like the Artist and Repertoire people do at record companies. That is, be an advocate for the songwriter

and help them navigate through any legal or other requirements)

Any one of these functions could be done by either the songwriting community or the publishing company. Share responsibilities according to your plans and skills. They could be accomplished under one "roof," but your company design is completely up to you. I'll provide the blueprint for the critical functions. No matter who or how, here are the goals:

- Educate and nurture solid and sought-after songwriters
- Write and deliver songs on how God is moving in your community
- Record and market the best songs to the wider world

Distribution to your local church communities is always the priority.

This list contains important topics for songwriter educational opportunities. If you are interested in songwriting community administration, take note to offer these for discussions and Q&A sessions.

GETTING ORGANIZED

Before you think this section is going to be full of boring legal talk and you're thinking of skipping it, commit to skimming it instead. I'll make it interesting for you, the songwriter. I'm going to show you how to copyright your songs. Also, I write a list of the royalty collection organizations where you need to register in 2022 and beyond.

This section will also speak to your inner-songwriting administration and publishing company geek. Show this to your friends who want to help you get your songs heard. After all, the goal is to build a faith-based song publishing *organization* that is fully aligned with, and dedicated to, the mission of the songwriting organization. And the songwriting organization is dedicated to the reputation and mission of the songwriter whose greater mission is to write songs that honor and glorify the Lord, and invite others to do the same.

> *It's time to distribute your important local theology songs to churches hungry for well-written songs of praise.*

It's time to distribute your important local theology songs to churches hungry for well-written songs of praise. The distribution model for the local area is the same vehicle used for the broader market.

Think about repeating a similar cycle of victory:

- Write or co-write a song
- Have it critiqued by the forum
- You and your writers improve the song
- You submit the song to the committee that decides on promoting them
- If you get a positive review, get a demo of the song recorded
- Have all chord charts prepared for it
- Songwriting organization leadership has the song registered in all the right places

- The organization promotes the song to churches and worship leaders
- The faith-based publisher promotes the song as a Spotify single, or
- Several of the recordings are added to a compilation or an EP
- The organization promotes and showcases your recorded music to regional and national bands and audiences

Now imagine scaling this model to promote 10 or more songs simultaneously while promoting these recordings to regional and national Christian bands and artists. Imagine creating a showcase for these songs and hiring a top band to perform them. You invite the media, music industry executives, and local, regional, and national church leadership. These would be worthy goals.

SPECIAL ADVANTAGES FOR CHURCH SONGWRITERS

You will find much more detail on the songwriting community and publishing company requirements in my book *Fishing in Church.* And there is another level of depth in my e-book *Worship Songs and the Law: How Churches Stay Legal and Songwriters Get Paid.* I want to encourage you to get both.

We have this extraordinary opportunity today because of events that took place forty years ago. Changes in US copyright law, restructured in 1976, and the birth of CCLI in 1984 have revolutionized the way music is distributed and used in churches. The songwriter is central to this revolutionary opportunity.

Those two major events change *everything* for the twenty-first century Christian songwriter. These inflection points brought clarity for church song legal compliance and benefits to rights holders never before seen.

Lawmakers inserted language into Title 17 of the US Code for how churches operate within copyright law. Section 110, Item 3 which declares this *is not* a violation of copyright law:

> *"PERFORMANCE of a nondramatic literary or musical work or of a dramatico-musical work of a religious nature, or DISPLAY of a work, in the course of services at a place of worship or other religious assembly."*

This means churches are exempt from the infringement that performance or the display of works used *during* services would otherwise cause. No previous language existed, and this new language emboldened music publishers to cry "infringement" when churches didn't comply. After the Archdiocese of Chicago had a pending $3.1 million copyright infringement lawsuit in 1984, specifically for the distribution of printed music and lyrics, CCLI was formed to issue licenses to churches. To prevent further lawsuits, CCLI came into agreement with the Record Industry Association of America and the major music publishers to offer to protect churches with these licenses and collect fees to pay for church use of songs.

These licenses cover member churches that copy music and lyrics *in preparation* for church services. Church workers all have *copies* of songs on their hard drives, in printed forms used for both practice and during church services, and sometimes distribute audio and print copies to members. Churches use video clips of movies during services and stream their worship services which further distributes performances and lyrics of copyrighted works. CCLI offers licenses to churches for all these situations.

CCLI is a unique form of a performance rights agency. These license fees also raise money for *independent* intellectual property rights holders, Christian songwriters and publishers that otherwise would not receive remuneration. They also provide programs and services for member publishers and churches as written in the *Introduction* of this book.

Church Copyright Solutions (notice the slightly different name) and other similar organizations offer licenses for the use of songs *outside* of services, such as music in coffee shops, music on hold, or copyrighted songs used by churches for prayer meetings and youth events.

This convergence of copyright law changes and the creation of CCLI give us the runway lights for how the Christian music publisher, small and large, operates today. Larger churches with songwriting communities know full well the ins and outs of copyright law, music publishing, CCLI, and song administration tasks (or they hire song administration companies and music lawyers to take care of these things for them). Your new faith-based local songwriting community and music publisher will also understand current practices and laws and will be dedicated to the grassroots small-church local theology revolution.

Songwriters, it is possible you will sign a contract with such an organization, so the information you will read in this section will be important to understand. Knowing your legal rights will take you far.

I want you to have peace of mind and know that your dream of writing songs and getting them "out there" is not only possible, but you have a clear path to make it happen. There will be people along the way who will want to help you blaze this new trail.

IT'S YOUR PUBLISHING UNTIL YOU GIVE IT AWAY

The first change in 1976 copyright law saw the establishment of *economic* property rights for songwriters. In that change a method was created so copyright holders could firmly establish their claim of ownership through the Library of Congress.

The United States was also interested in joining the Berne Convention, an international copyright body with multiple nation members, which it eventually did in 1989. A stipulation of the Berne Convention was that they add "*a copyright is established when an author places a work in fixed form*" language to our law. This was agreed-upon international language, meaning that the copyright holder established *moral* rights in the work the moment the work is expressed.

The US added this language in 1976, but in true capitalistic form greatly expanded copyright law to include a path for the intellectual property (IP) rights holder to establish *economic* rights and a pathway to protect those rights.

The intrinsic *moral* rights were also established, but are only legally defensible through the economic protection pathway.

Even though the following information applies to the US, this information is relevant to songwriters and music publishers everywhere. Copyright law is similar in every country.

You need to know the rights you have as a song creator and how to protect these rights in the US. I won't cloud your brain with details of the law, but you should know the basics of copyright law as it pertains to song ownership. I talk about copyright law basics, hoping you have a desire to learn more. I'm not selling fear and clouds, I'm selling that knowledge is power.

You own the publishing rights on your song, and the copyright itself, until you give those rights away. Contract offers from publishing companies are all about you signing over these rights.

> *You own the publishing rights on your song, and the copyright itself, until you give those rights away. Contract offers from publishing companies are all about you signing over these rights.*

Remember: The point of this section isn't to bore you with legal facts and jargon. It is to make you familiar with what you own when you write a song. You should always consult a lawyer for the best information and for what is best for your situation.

Your rights under copyright law:

- The right to reproduce the work.
- The right to distribute the work in various forms, e.g., print, digital, physical.

- The right to prepare derivative works.
- The right to display the work in public.
- The right to perform the work publicly.
- The right to transmit the work digitally (sound recording only).

PROTECT YOUR PROPERTY

US law establishes a path for economic justice for the registered copyright owner. Moral claims without evidence of ownership don't hold the same weight in the law. However, moral rights are protected by taking the same song registration pathway.

Ok. You've placed your work in a fixed form. Morally, according to the Berne Convention and the US Code, that's all you need to establish ownership of the work. However, to protect your work, you need to register your copyright with the US Copyright Office to *enforce your economic rights.*

I understand the anxiety that is produced when you feel that a person has either stolen your song or is using it without your permission, but the only reason for litigation is to establish monetary rights to the IP. The initial statement in the US Code, "…in a fixed form" should be enough to enforce your claim, right?

It is not.

You wouldn't want to take someone to court because of your moral claim. You won't be successful. Is it because they stole your song and are making money, or is it on the principle that it's yours? The difference between the two is an economic argument versus a moral one.

US law establishes a path for economic justice for the registered copyright owner. Moral claims without evidence of ownership don't hold the same weight in the law. However, moral rights are protected by taking the same song registration pathway.

The bottom line is that if you want to protect your work, then you will follow the copyright registration procedures found at https://copyright.gov. In particular, read Copyrights Basics Circular 1, https://www.copyright.gov/circs/circ01.pdf. Here's a quote from page 4 under the heading, *How Can I Protect My Work?*

> *The bottom line is that if you want to protect your work, then you will follow the copyright registration procedures found at https://copyright.gov.*

*Copyright exists automatically in an original work of authorship once it is fixed in a tangible medium, but a copyright owner can take steps to enhance the protections of copyright, the most important of which is registering the work. **Although registering a work is not mandatory, for US works, registration (or refusal) is necessary to enforce the exclusive rights of copyright through litigation.***

Emphasis in the above quote is mine. (Side note on **refusal**—if you submit an application for a copyright and it is refused, the copyright office will recognize your right to instigate litigation against an infringer, even though your application was rejected. More details in §411 of USC Title 17.)

The US has created a solution to help document your creation. This method creates a way to identify the true owner of a work. Also, this solution goes hand in hand with any potential litigation in the US court system. Meaning, this method of registering can create an open-and-shut legal case to protect your work.

You can register the song with the US Copyright Office, a division of the Library of Congress. When you do this, you submit a copy of the work and establish authorship and publishing rights. They will send you a copyright registration in the mail.

Your song is registered with them the moment you submit your Performance Arts application online and pay the fee.

What You Get When You Register for a US Copyright:

1. A signed Certificate of Registration with a Registration Number and Effective Date of Registration. This constitutes a legal witness from a government institution of your authorship and ownership of all publishing rights.

2. *Prima facie* (face value) evidence of the validity of the copyright and the facts on the certificate if registered within five years of publication.

    a. If the song is registered within three months of the date of authorship, you're automatically eligible to receive statutory damages and legal fees from any infringer.

    b. There's no automatic right to receive the damages and fees if the song is registered at a date later than three months. This doesn't preclude the possibility that a judge might not see your side of the story.

3. The work is protected for the life of the author plus seventy years (a part of US copyright law, not a specific right from the US Copyright Office. This part of the law is sealed in the eyes of the court when you register your song).

The above benefits are taken from *Copyright Basics Circular 1*.

If you decide that someone has copied your work and made money, you're in a much better position to take them to court. The government circular on copyright states that having a registration is a *requirement* before you can begin litigation.

WHAT IF I DON'T REGISTER WITH THE COPYRIGHT OFFICE?

Other legal sites say you *can* begin litigation without a copyright registration because of the moral rights written into copyright law. You can, but your request will be substantially limited. Translation: is it smart to begin litigation without government registration?

- No government witness as to authorship
- No *prima facie* evidence of your authorship (you must prove everything)
- No automatic right to receive damages and fees from the litigator

That's a pretty huge set of limitations. Always seek legal counsel to understand your options.

See all the FAQs at https://www.copyright.gov/help/faq/index.html. You can register your copyright at any time, but it's only during the stated window that you automatically receive the added protection and fee payment guarantees.

WHY ARE YOU TAKING THE INFRINGER TO COURT?

Remember you most likely wouldn't be in court unless the other side was making money from your work.

Recognize the right form of action to take and decide if it's worth pursuing.

The first right action:

If you believe someone is violating copyright law and publishing your work, you need to file a *cease-and-desist* order. You can find one on the internet or hire a lawyer to do this for you. This order proclaims the work is yours and demands that the user stop their actions, including the recall of any copies of your works.

Your notice will have the weight of the US Copyright Office behind it. And it will deliver a heavy punch when you tell them you've registered the song in a timely manner, and they will bear the cost

The other party will be impressed that you've taken these steps. They'll comply or they'll ignore you. If they ignore you, there are two choices: Appeal to them in person (whether through a lawyer or yourself) or take them to court.

of any statutory damages and fees awarded by the court should they lose the case.

Your court case will have a much greater chance of succeeding.

The other party will be impressed that you've taken these steps. They'll comply or they'll ignore you. If they ignore you, there are two choices: Appeal to them in person (whether through a lawyer or yourself) or take them to court.

If the other side has done their homework and found out you do not actually have a registration from the Library of Congress, they will ignore your *cease-and-desist* order. It's time to do *your* homework using the US Copyright Office Public Catalog to see if they have made a registration: https://cocatalog.loc.gov/cgi-bin/Pwebrecon.cgi?DB=local&PAGE=First

If you proceed with the lawsuit, they will *most likely* win the case if *they* have registered the work and you haven't.

Unless you can prove to the judge—beyond any doubt—that your work was stolen *and* you have a *timely* registration, you may not have much of a chance. But, hey, I'm not a judge.

Maybe you decide you have a good enough case to instigate litigation. Just know that the party responsible for legal fees is not a cut-and-dried issue for infringement cases in the US court system. https://alj.artrepreneur.com/fees-fair-supreme-court-copyright-law/

Are you prepared for these challenges?

Why not just register your songs with the US Copyright Office in the first place? I understand it can be about money. But if you feel there's any chance your song could be stolen, well … just do it.

THE POOR MAN'S COPYRIGHT MYTH

If you don't have a registration, do you have proof that the underlying creation, the words and music, is your work? Will a "poor man's copyright" work (mailing yourself a copy so it has a date stamped on the envelope)?

Nope.

This method will not persuade a judge because dates can be faked, according to numerous sources. The FAQ page of copyright division at the Library of Congress says it's not a substitute for a registration.

What if the date is verified by a third party?

Other copyright registration firms do this. They are in business to make this proof-of-date stamping, like what is intended with the "poor man's copyright," legitimate. Do these firms, with a product often referred to as an "internet copyright," provide good enough protection for a court of law?

No. Do they provide a legal date stamp of your work? Yes … but only if a judge agrees that piece of evidence is valid for *your particular case.*

You see, these other firms are literally banking on the first chapter of copyright law, which states that you have a legal copyright when you place it in a fixed form. Their opinion is that's enough. Period. No other proof is necessary, they say, because the rest of the laws are scare tactics. Or the government is trying to make money.

These other firms are the ones trying to make that money, and the return on your investment is not good.

All of them may be good for creating a date stamp of your work, and that work and date stamp is hosted by them, an eye witness for your court case. But …

- Will they be present in court when you need them?
- Do they guarantee the judge will see your claim of authorship as legitimate?
- Can they guarantee the infringer must pay statutory damages and legal fees?

Good questions to ask them. Do the right research before sending your money anywhere. Read their fine print. *In every case*, they will state that their service is not a substitute for a copyright registration from the US Copyright Office.

LIFE OF THE AUTHOR PLUS 70 YEARS

My answer to the above three questions is "No." These companies all fall short of the protection provided by the Library of Congress. *They do not offer monetary or ownership protection.*

US copyright law states the rightful owner of the copyright has protection under the law for the life of the author plus 70 years.

> *US copyright law states the rightful owner of the copyright has protection under the law for the life of the author plus 70 years.*

Are you willing to go bargain hunting to shop for "copyright protection"—gambling with this guarantee under the law—at another business when you understand the government option?

What happens when, not if, these companies go out of business?

Are you willing to forego the statutory life-of-the-author-plus-70-years clause, over saving a few dollars?

> (**Author's note**: Again, the 70-year clause is a section of US copyright law. But the timely registration of your song with them guarantees not only the right for you to claim statutory damages and legal fees, it cements this 70-year clause in your favor in the eyes of a judge. If you allow another party to register a claim on your song, *they* get the 70-year guarantee. See Copyright Basics Circular 1 https://www.copyright.gov/circs/circ01.pdf).

Here's what the US Copyright Office will *not* do for you: They will not put up the money so you can begin your case. That's all on you. If you've filed a timely registration with them, you can recover statutory damages and fees, and then pay off your lawyers.

MY BOTTOM LINE

Should you send for a copyright registration for every song that you write? That would be up to you. But I'd recommend you do that for *any* song you've distributed on the internet, or for any song you've created for a demo or an album.

Remember: One of the rights as a copyright owner is *the right to first publication* of your work. If you post your work on the internet, or hand out copies, you have essentially published the song. If you've done that without protecting the song and an infringer registers this work, you can say goodbye to any other rights you think you have.

THE STATEMENT FROM THE ELEPHANT IN THE ROOM

"Look, Steve. Nobody needs to worry about getting their songs registered. The publisher will take care of that. *Publishers* might do it all the time to protect their IP, but I don't need to. Nobody cares about my songs until there's money involved. So, it's ok for me to just pay the lower fees and get my songs registered with these other companies."

My response: *Oh, really?* The US government creates a legal fortress to protect your personal property. Yet you want to play with fire and let someone steal your work so they can build *their* fortress around it?

I'll take the protection the US government provides for my song, thank you. It is not only guaranteed money in case of infringement, but also the perfect setup to make an announcement to would-be thieves.

Accept no substitute.

Author Note: Buried in the enormous COVID stimulus relief bill of December 2020, Congress passed a small claims court for copyright infringement claims: https://www.jdsupra.com/legalnews/ congress-creates-a-small-claims-court-7022155/

PROS AND PERFORMANCE ROYALTIES

"Money won't create success, the freedom to make it will."

Nelson Mandela

Before I go any further, I want to tell you that I know how confusing the talk of royalties, music publishing, copyright, etc. is to the layperson. Hey, it is massively confusing even to those who live it or have done a ton of research (me). I want you to know that I am *not* trying to explain the entire song royalty distribution mess to you. *I only care to share what's pertinent to songwriting and songs used in church.*

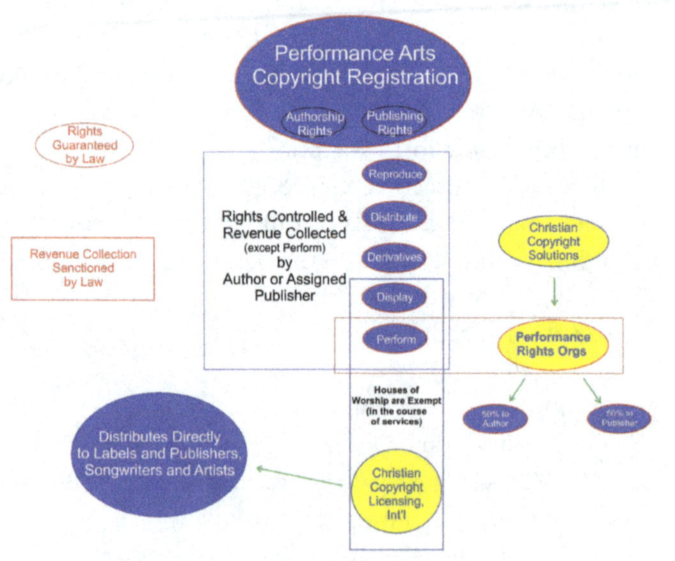

Song publishing and revenue for the
congregational songwriter

The graphic above tells the entire royalty and copyright story I wish to tell.

For all the points that I previously made about songs used in church, getting a song copyright, and for all the points I will make regarding PROs and publishers going forward, refer to this chart when points get confusing. The main points of the chart above are these:

1. CCLI pays songwriters, artists, and copyright holders *directly* for royalties due them for the display, copying, distribution, and streaming of their IP by member churches.

2. Three PROs in the US—see which three in the section *PRO for Christian music* below—pay 50% to the authors, and 50% to the publishers of record their share of royalties due for use of their IP *outside* of church services.

Come back and view this chart often as you continue reading. Let this visual inform the big picture of what we want to accomplish, getting our congregational songs heard and how we will use the system to build our ministries.

It's my hope that this graphic helps to fill in the knowledge gap as I explain what's on my heart. You will find this graphic and multiple graphics as the song rights and royalty picture develops in my books *Fishing in Church* and *Worship Songs and the Law: How Churches Stay Legal and Songwriters Get Paid*. Although I go into more detail in those books, the focus remains on songwriting and songs used in church.

The publisher, or the individual, owns the *exclusive* rights to public performance or digital transmission of their work. They legally control the terms of that right.

However, they do not control or initiate the fees charged or the money collected when those rights are exercised. PROs manage public performance money in the US.

Copyright law in the US mandates the collection of performance fees by the PROs. Two of them, the American Society of Composers, Authors and Publishers (ASCAP) and Broadcast Music Incorporated (BMI), are non-profit. Society of European Stage Authors and Composers (SESAC) and Global Music Rights (GMR) are for-profit with membership by invitation only.

There is a new US PRO as of 2019, AllTrack, built specifically for independent music creators. It boasts that the member automatically receives royalties from over 120 countries using a special digital platform.

SoundExchange is also a PRO mandated by US Congress, but strictly for the collection and distribution of fees and royalties for digital *sound recordings*. It is an organization where you register your works, however, it is not the same as the others. The others might offer both digital and non-digital royalty collections, but SoundExchange only offers the collection of digital.

HOW PERFORMANCE RIGHTS ROYALTY COLLECTION WORKS

Each country has its own PRO. In most other countries, the PRO collects all forms of fees and royalties. But in the US, only public performance fees are collected, and royalties distributed.

The PROs issue licenses to restaurants, bars and clubs, performance venues of different sizes, malls and office buildings that play Muzak, etc. The fees paid depend on the size of a place, the occupancy, and how often and how many works are performed.

The money the PROs collect is split 50/50, by law, to the songwriter of record and to the publisher of record. How do they know who these people are? *The holder of the copyright must register their songs with them.*

If you have a signed contract with a publisher, that company will register the song (or re-register the song) with your PRO. They'll document you as the author and the company as the publisher of record.

For anyone who is self-published, it's your responsibility to register the song as the author and as the publisher of record.

The funds collected by the PRO are divvied up and distributed *directly* to the author and the publisher of record *separately* because that's also mandated by law. The PRO will distribute after subtracting their fees.

> *If you have a signed contract with a publisher, that company will register the song (because they are the holder of the copyright). They'll document you as the author and the company as the publisher of record.*

For example, ASCAP reported in 2018 they returned 90% of all monies collected to songwriters and publishers.

The industry speaks about the *performance royalty split* this way:

There are two pies. The first whole pie is authorship. You and your co-writers own 100% of the pie. The second whole pie is money generated by publishing rights. You and your co-writers own 100% of that pie, too.

You would be leaving money on the table if you did not register your songs with a PRO. If your songs generate interest and are performed or recorded by others, they need to be registered with a PRO so performance credits can be calculated.

SIGN UP WITH A PRO

Sign up today with ASCAP, BMI, SESAC or AllTrack.

It's very simple—pick one. You can only sign up for one of the PROs as a writer. Each organization has its own membership criteria. Music publishing companies can sign up with all the PROs because they sign writers who are members of each of them.

I recommend signing up with the PRO as a songwriter and publisher at the same time. The reason is that you control the publishing on your songs. When you register them as both the songwriter and publisher, you'll be able to collect both royalty payments. A new development to this industry practice is that AllTrack automatically signs you up for both if you're a self-published writer.

While venues are responsible for paying fees to the PROs, you (or your publisher) are responsible for reporting your songs to them to get credit.

WHICH PRO?

Register your songs to be ready to receive performance royalties. Pick a PRO and sign up with one today. ASCAP allows it and recommends it. BMI says, "Don't bother until you can prove performances." And SESAC says, "Do it. Do you know that we'll pay royalties no matter the public venue where your song is performed? All you need to do is report it." AllTrack clearly wants to sign new talent. GMR isn't talking. They are a more closed society for industry professionals.

If you're performing your own material in front of increasingly larger crowds, you should consider becoming a member of one of the PROs and register your songs with them. You can report these performances to your PRO and receive credit.

> *If you're performing your own material in front of increasingly larger crowds, you should consider becoming a member of one of the PROs and register your songs with them.*

Here's a list of the PROs in the US:

- ASCAP
- BMI
- SESAC
- GMR
- AllTrack
- SoundExchange

SoundExchange—and remember that you can only register sound recordings with them—only collects and distributes revenue generated by non-interactive digital services (e.g., you can't decide what is played next: Satellite, Sirius XM, Pandora, etc.)

AllTrack advertises that they track plays and collect revenue from digital streaming companies like Spotify, Apple Music, YouTube, Rhapsody, etc., a first among US PROs. Streaming is considered performance. The royalties are split 50/50 between mechanical (the reproduction of a work whether it is physical or digital) and performance.

The streaming services pay the publishing companies through the Harry Fox Agency and to independent songwriters directly.

A change in US law, effective January 1, 2021, is the creation of the Mechanical License Collective. They collect fees from streaming services and distribute them to independent songwriters directly, while the Harry Fox Agency collects and distributes for larger music companies.

PRO FOR CHRISTIAN MUSIC

Christian songwriters have an additional organization where they can register and from where they can receive royalty payments: CCLI. But they are not a PRO, they are a service organization that collects revenue from churches copying, displaying, distributing, and streaming IP.

As mentioned earlier, there is also another major licensing organization called Christian Copyright Solutions, Inc (CCS). They collect fees from churches for the use of songs *outside* of services. They pay the proceeds to three PROs in the US—ASCAP, BMI, and SESAC—who in turn distribute the monies to their affiliated writers and publishers.

Yet another important reason to choose and sign up with a PRO. If you are congregational songwriter in the US, I suggest choosing one of those three PROs.

So, to recap: In the US, songwriters can register with and receive performance royalty payments from one of the PROs and from CCLI. CCS licenses churches and sends money to ASCAP, BMI, and SESAC from their license fee income for eventual distribution to rights holders.

For the differences between CCLI and CCS, please see this page: https://christiancopyrightsolutions.com/

learning-center/. See my special report *Worship Songs and the Law: How Churches Stay Legal and Songwriters Get Paid* at https://amazon.com/author/stephenrobertcass for a more in-depth review of CCLI, CCS, and songs used in church.

WORSHIP SONGWRITER ACTION LIST

Here's how to prepare and register now for royalty payments. The Music Modernization Act of 2018 mandated the creation of a central database to identify and match sound recordings to rights holders so they can be paid mechanical royalties. The database is being built and managed by the Mechanical License Collective (MLC), which was funded by the digital music services, and has been in place since January 1, 2021, at https://themlc.com.

See https://en.wikipedia.org/wiki/Music_Modernization_Act.

The effect of this new law is to simplify the fees collected and royalties paid for mechanical licensing and digital transmissions of songs.

Here's the list of what you need to do today:

- Place all of your songs in a spreadsheet with information such as:
  - Song name
  - Co-writer names
  - Songwriter split percentages (ownership)
  - Songwriter PRO affiliation
  - All IPI numbers (Interested Party Information given to songwriters, composers, and publishers issued by PROs)

- ○ ISWC (International Standard Musical Code) and ISRC (International Standard Recording Code)
- ○ CCLI song number

This spreadsheet is the beginning of your song catalog.

- Sign up with a PRO to capture any public performances of your works and to be prepared for others to record and perform your work. If you are a congregational songwriter in the US you should choose ASCAP, BMI, or SESAC. CCS collects money for your songs used outside of church services and pays them directly to those three PROs, who in turn pays their songwriting and publishing affiliates.
- Sign up with SoundExchange and list any sound recordings you own. If you have a record contract, the company owns these sound recordings (that is, unless you have another deal) and will register the works.
- List your digital works with streaming services. This is done automatically with CDBaby, Spotify, and whatever company you choose when you send your works for duplication or digital distribution. Obtain ISRC numbers independently or from those who distribute your digital recording, and ISWC numbers independently or from your PRO as you register the work. You'll need these numbers for the next step. Here's a great site explaining these codes. https://blog.songtradr.com/what-are-iswc-isrc-codes-and-how-do-i-get-them/

- Become a member of a *Digital Rights Reproduction Collection Agency* (DRCA) such as Audiam, TuneCore, CDBabyPro, or Songtrust. Each of these offer song publishing administration agreements, but the important reason is you'll register your ISRC numbers with them so they can collect and distribute royalties for the underlying composition, for your authorship. Remember, you don't receive money from these entities for sales.

If you're in the US, you can sign up with the MLC instead of a DRCA. It's either the MLC or one of the DRCAs, not both. Here are the major differences:

- The MLC only covers collecting and distributing streaming royalties in the US
- Other DRCAs collect streaming royalties internationally, including the US
- The MLC is absolutely free of charge.
- Other DRCAs have fees and take a percentage of any royalty money received for their services.

Notes: Ok, it's time to make this clear. As an artist, you choose some company like DistroKid or CDBaby to distribute your digital product. The royalties you collect from them are from the *sales* of your product.

CDBaby and TuneCore *also* have DRCA sign-ups for the collection of mechanical streaming and download fees from Spotify, Apple Music, Rhapsody, and others. You'll recognize this from the terms CDBabyPro and TuneCore Publishing. They're selling you extra publishing administration services. These services pay royalties to rights holders for the *underlying composition (authorship)*.

As a scenario, choose CDBaby for creating and hosting the song *only*. Then choose Songtrust as a publishing administration firm and a DRCA for that song (or choose the MLC for the song instead of the DRCA, Songtrust).

More Notes: As your song list grows, the above is a good exercise in helping you organize and update your catalog. Though it's confusing at first, it's also excellent knowledge about the type of royalties payable to you. Don't get caught up in the FOMO. Make the DRCA decision with a clear head according to your goals and desires.

You'll want to sign up with one of the DRCAs listed if you are an artist or songwriter with a worldwide reach. Evaluate the cost compared with the amount of royalties you expect to receive. But my advice is to stop. Breathe. Understand your priorities as a congregational songwriter.

CONGREGATIONAL SONGWRITER PRIORITIES

I would consider signing up for the free option (if you live in the US), the MLC, as a songwriter with the primary concern of *making Jesus famous* and getting your songs out to local churches. You can always decide to sign up for a larger international publishing administration strategy with a DRCA if your songs generate worldwide recognition.

> *It is important for the congregational songwriter to have their song registered with CCLI. They exist to distribute your songs to over 250,000 churches around the world.*

It is important for the congregational songwriter to have their song registered with CCLI, who collects fees from churches and distributes royalties for rights holders. They are the largest Christian song lyric and sheet music publisher in the world. *They exist to distribute your songs to over 250,000 churches around the world.*

You may not be able to sign up with CCLI as an individual unless you have multiple songs and a planned reach for those songs. You can sign with your new, local, faith-based publisher who has a publisher membership with CCLI. Even if you already have an individual publisher membership with CCLI and you become a member of the new, local, faith-based publisher, the right agreements will be in place to assure accountability and integrity.

Finally, I want to remind you to choose ASCAP, BMI, or SESAC as your PRO. These entities authorize CCS to license churches and ministries to perform and play the songs in their catalogs, and in turn pay their affiliated songwriters and publishers.

WHAT DOES A PUBLISHER DO?

"Constant endeavor plus management amounts to success"

G. S. Alag

The word "exploitation" often has a negative connotation. All opinions aside, publishing companies do not set out to steal the work from music creators. There has to be a descriptor for the actions taken by them, and that's the word. Merriam-Webster defines exploitation as "to make productive use of or to utilize." Basically, publishers find uses for songs. The company has a contract with the authors of the songs, the creators, who sign their publishing rights over to them. A publisher "exploits" these rights. They're in the business of getting others to buy and use the song, for a price, of course.

The holder of the publishing rights, whether a publishing company or an individual, collects and distributes (if needed) any revenue generated by the song—except fees generated by physical and digital performances, which I covered as the domain of the PRO in the US

So, that's their goal—to make money for the company and the songwriter. The usual deal is for the company to own 25% or 50% of the publishing rights of the song or songs. They make other percentage deals all the time, but the bottom line is that they now want to have the *exclusive* right to exploit the song or songs. They find any kind of use for the song, including:

- Publish and license sheet music.
- Find other artists and publishers interested in recording your songs (for example, uses in film, TV, and video games).
- Administer the song catalog.
- Protect the songs by registering copyrights (in the US).
- Register the songs to receive performance royalties.
- Collect, account for, and distribute exploitation royalties.

Note: The one who holds the copyright, usually the publishing company, controls the rights of *public performance*. But again, they don't control or collect that money. They are still responsible, though, to register the song with the PRO of the songwriter so the publisher(s) and author(s) are on record.

SHOW ME THE MONEY

There are two money pies from the publishing rights:

- Performance and
- Exploitation of the other exclusive rights
  - The right to reproduce the work.
  - The right to distribute the work in various forms, e.g., print, digital, physical.
  - The right to prepare derivative works.
  - The right to display the work in public.

The *authors* of the song receive 100% of the author's share of **performance** royalties, paid to them directly by the PROs for the authors of record. The PROs also pay 100% of the publisher's share of **performance** royalties directly to the *publisher* of record, by US law.

What the publisher does with performance money is their business. And you need to read about it in your contract. Some publishers will keep all this income.

But see "the *performance* money pie": 100% of authorship money, 100% of publisher money = a 50/50 *performance* royalty split. Always. That percentage will never change (it's not controlled by the publisher, but by US copyright law).

The next money pie is income from *exploitations*. This revenue is generated by the publishing company.

The publishing company is liable, under contract, to pay you, the songwriter 50% (or whatever percentage they negotiated with you) of all monies received for any exploitation of the songs. But they are **not** liable to pay you any income that they receive legally, separately, from performance royalties.

Different percentage deals are on the table all the time. The deal that will be given to you is about the publisher's share of each right owned in a song or songs. Remember, the creator owns 100% of the publishing share until signed over.

WHAT INCOME IS RECEIVED FROM EXPLOITATION?

- Print and digital sales of sheet music
  - Individual sheet music and folios

- Mechanical reproduction licenses
  - Others who want to record your song pay a mechanical reproduction fee

- Synchronization licenses for film and TV
  - Broadcasters pay for the use of the underlying work

- Grand Rights
  - When your music is used on the drama stage

- Foreign Royalties
  - Royalties and usage fees collected outside your country

- Unforeseen collections
- Income from exploitation not on this list or from technology yet known

You may notice music industry revenue is missing from this list: Income from record sales and distribution, and income from digital sales and streaming. Those income streams are usually from record companies and digital sales platforms, respectively, not publishing companies.

What will a real publishing company never do?

A bona fide publisher will *never* ask for any money up front from you. If any company asks for money up front, it's because they're primarily in business to do something else—like create demos.

> *A bona fide publisher will never ask for any money up front from you. If any company asks for money up front, it's because they're primarily in business to do something else—like create demos.*

Some legitimate publishing companies are in business to create demos, but most of the time demos are often your job to pay for and create, depending on your deal with them. If you sign a staff-writer contract, then they'll create and pay for the demos. While you'll always be known as the songwriter in this circumstance, you'll have no publishing rights because the work you do will be *work made for hire.*

Again, read the fine print. They make different deals all the time.

Some companies, like TAXI, a song service found at https://taxi.com, are in business to find placements for your song with record labels, publishers, music libraries, and film & TV music supervisors *only.* They don't want your publishing rights. You're hiring them for a job that doesn't require you giving away the rights to your songs.

WHAT DOES THIS PUBLISHER DO?

"Every right implies a responsibility; Every opportunity, an obligation, Every possession, a duty."

John D. Rockefeller

Now the question becomes not only what do publishing companies do, what does *this* publishing company do, your new faith-based music publisher?

I'm excited to share this with you, but I know that organizing isn't everyone's cup of tea. I am proud of you for becoming a congregational songwriter, no matter how you feel about the organization part. If you are only interested in becoming a songwriter for the church, I'm happy. You'll have a skill unmatched in the world of songwriting. I would ask that you pass this information on to those songwriters in your church, in your town, who might be interested in organizing.

You need a faith-based publisher to be assured you have a team looking out for your best interest. The songwriting organization needs a faith-based publisher to be certain that their writers and their songs have the best possible representation and protection.

There can be a great number of details involved, but they will flow naturally between songwriters and song administrators, and from your commitment to common goals.

The idea is: This is *your* business. You don't have to learn how to be someone else's version of a publisher or record company to do this.

WHAT YOU HAVE

This is IP that belongs to you and the other songwriters. Your songs need proper legal protection and exploitation. The creator of the song holds all publishing rights:

- The right to reproduce the work
- The right to distribute the work in various forms
    - print, digital, physical

- The right to prepare derivative works
- The right to display the work in public
- The right to perform the work publicly
- The right to transmit the work digitally (sound recording only)

As a leadership group, you'll need to decide which songs need full copyright protection. My suggestion is that you copyright them in groups as unpublished works first, when you make demos, but it is always up to you. Maybe you're excited about a great song, and you will get full protection. Choose full copyrights on songs you plan to publish and distribute.

THE HILLSONG PUBLISHING MODEL

The Hillsong Publishing company plan contains the nucleus of a well-managed, well-focused music business for any faith-based organization. It's worth exploring how their model works, then modifying it to form your own plan.

Here's the URL to the document that Steve McPherson, the manager of Hillsong Publishing, wrote on how they

administer and publish their music: https://songs4god.net/
wp-content/uploads/2020/08/Copyright-and-Music-
Publishing-in-the-Church.pdf.

At the heart of this model is the decision by the
organization to take the responsibility of administering the
songs of their writers. This ownership carries with it the
duty of creating awareness and usage of the songs.

All the songwriters at Hillsong assign the publishing
rights to Hillsong Publishing. The songwriters are paid
the author portion of performance royalties directly from
the PROs. The publisher portion of the royalty goes to
Hillsong Church. The same is true of all CCLI royalties;
they are paid directly to Hillsong Church. Although it's
difficult to find any certain money plan from them, articles
such as the following state as much as my declaration in this
paragraph: https://au.rollingstone.com/music/music-news/
inside-hillsong-church-hit-making-music-machine-6661/

KEEP IT SIMPLE

Before I expand on this nucleus, take a step back and view
the six publishing rights of the creator in the above list. The
writer of the song holds these rights unless they assign them
to a publishing company. This also means they hold the
following *exclusive* rights to:

- Record and distribute the song
- Seek other opportunities for the song to be
  recorded (other record companies and artists)
- Find uses in film and television
- Print and distribute lyrics, chord charts, and
  lead sheets

- Collect fees and royalties for the uses of the song
- Legally protect the work
- Register the work with the US Copyright Office, PROs, digital rights organizations, and CCLI

If the organization wished to record and find uses for the song, it's the responsibility of the writer to execute all the contracts necessary to allow the use of their property in the above circumstances. Any other imagined uses of the song can only be done with written permission from the songwriter. This adds layers of complication. It can be done, and I'll show you how. But first I want to continue with the model I recommend.

SHARE YOUR NEW COMMITMENT

Think of the publishing/record label functions as a division of the songwriting organization. The publishing division will commit to the administration and exploitation of the songs so the songwriting division can concentrate on writing songs.

Now it's time to share this decision. Shout it from the rooftop with your writers! Have that initial conversation with them regarding the plans for your organization. Also share your enthusiasm that dividing the organization between songwriting and publishing will only increase the efforts on both sides.

Talk with them about royalty collections and exactly what to expect. Establish full and transparent negotiations and draft publishing contracts.

Please consult an entertainment attorney with your contract ideas.

Here's your short list of commitments. You can adopt this list as goals for your publishing division:

- Release records in a steady flow.
- Promote the reputation of the organization as "on a mission" in press releases or ads.
- Promote the same "on a mission" goals to the songwriters. And the message of how you'll accomplish the goals.
- Administer the song catalog.
- Apply for song copyrights with the Library of Congress (in the US).
- Register the songs with CCLI, the PROs and digital rights agencies to receive royalties.
- Collect and distribute royalties.
- Find song exploitations.
- Publish and license sheet music.
- Find other artists and publishers interested in recording your songs.
- Explore song uses in film, TV, and other entertainment.

> *The publishing division supports the main goals of the songwriting organization. It doesn't engage in music business that doesn't further the central cause of the songwriting organization. Be sure to search your soul regularly.*

The publishing division supports the main goals of the songwriting organization. It doesn't become its own entity (unless that's your legal design. Consult an attorney with your plans), and *it doesn't engage in music business that doesn't further the central cause of the songwriting organization. Be sure to search your soul regularly.*

THE DUTY OF A PUBLISHER

When you choose the path of a music publisher, you are creating an organization that is committed to lead and manage the publishing rights of songwriters to the best of their ability. You believe in the strength of your best songs and have faith that God will put them into the hands of worship leaders who will want to sing them in their churches.

Managing publishing rights comes with a heavy responsibility of finding exploitation opportunities, and that's ok. Be at the forefront and actively pursue the best interest of the songwriter so your organization thrives and grows, and so your organization is known for quality worship material for the glory of God.

Again, don't let your lack of knowledge stop you from creating this songwriting community. The primary consideration is for blessing local congregations with great songs and discovering great songwriters.

You don't have to build your music company to any certain level or to anyone else's expectation. Start small, start simply. But you should be aware that there are certain realities in dealing with the IP of others. You and your team can use this information to build your organization to the level you desire. Study more about how record and distribution organizations operate and adapt a model that best fits your goals.

Decide the aspects of the business in which you'll seek professional counsel, hire administration help, and seek volunteer input. No matter what you decide for publishing and administration, document your plans and write out your contracts. Take all contracts to an entertainment attorney for their review and advice.

THE SONGWRITING ORGANIZATION CONTROLS THE RIGHTS

To keep it simple and so it's best managed for all, I recommend that your song organization follows the same basic nucleus as the Hillsong model and execute the necessary contracts to control all publishing rights of the song(s).

> *To keep it simple and so it's best managed for all, I recommend that your song organization follows the same basic nucleus as the Hillsong model and execute the necessary contracts to control all publishing rights of the song(s).*

There are a few things the organization needs to communicate to songwriters before entering a partnership with them. First of all, the organization should make the songwriter keenly aware of their publishing rights. They should also assure the songwriter that they know how to manage those rights and how to find uses for songs.

Further, to properly manage the rights and eliminate the need for the songwriter to execute any contracts to use their IP, it should be communicated to them that it would be in their best interest to allow the organization to be the publisher of record and execute all contracts.

Having this understanding early on will remove all doubts about song representation. The writer needs to know that the organization will be the champion for them, and for all their songwriters, and will take full publishing responsibility—find every use possible and be the exclusive administrator—for their songs.

Assure the songwriter that you intend to do all the leg work necessary to make their songs widely available at the beginning of your relationship. Let them know that you promise to legally protect their work, promote their reputation and their integrity as a writer, and that you will represent and promote the songwriting organization with the same fervor. Yes, this is a serious responsibility. Take it head-on.

WHAT HAPPENS IF THE SONGWRITER KEEPS THEIR PUBLISHING RIGHTS?

If you decide songwriter members can keep their publishing rights, yet you still wish to record them, *and I do not recommend this*, this is the decision you have made:

- Your organization is for songwriting development and recording only.
- You might have an agreement with the writer about CCLI administration and royalty collection, but the only other responsibility of the organization is to pay the songwriters for any sales or royalties associated with the recordings.
- The only publishing rights you will own are for the IP of the sound recordings.

- The organization may own the recordings but will still need to have separate agreements and pay mechanical royalties to songwriters for the use of their songs in any compilations.
- The songwriters will have to initiate any other uses for their songs.
- The responsibility of the organization ends with any sort of recording agreement. It would be the responsibility of the writer to seek any other uses by artists or record companies, to register the work with any authorities, to seek legal counsel, and to chase any royalty payments.

> *The health of the organization requires thought to keep the legalities simple; to make the relationships stable so they stay focused on the goals of creating strong songwriters and quality songs for churches, not focused on money and individual responsibilities and rights.*

In short, you're telling the songwriter that the organization will not be their champion to protect the rights of their songs, and the organization exists only to help develop them as songwriters. Maybe you will be their publishing administrator for CCLI, but that's the extent of the relationship. If you want to be a record label and distribute *your* records with *their* songs, there will be a lot of extra paperwork, conversations, and legal fees.

There are ways to make the best of your situation. All individual publishing rights are negotiable, and you can create legal contracts to accomplish any goal.

The reason I don't recommend this path is that I believe it goes against the simple goal of banding together to get songs out to churches. The health of the organization requires thought to keep the legalities simple; to make the relationships stable so they stay focused on the goals of creating strong songwriters and quality songs for churches, not focused on money and individual responsibilities and rights. What's more, there's less chance for rivalry and division.

That said, there are still ways to work through any publishing and recording situation, no matter the legal challenge. But here's my bottom line:

> *The vast majority of songwriters won't seek uses for their songs. They only want to see their songs do well. They need your publishing company to represent their best interests and help get the best exploitations.*

Whenever you're faced with a decision, ask if the outcome would align with your primary goals. Here they are again:

- Educate and nurture solid and sought-after songwriters.
- Write and deliver songs on how God is moving in your community.
- Record and market the best songs to the wider world.

Your new music company is a combination of a songwriting organization and a publisher/record label. From here forward, I will refer to it as your new publishing company, but it will have many of the functions of a record label.

AGREEMENTS WITH THE SONGWRITERS

What I'm referring to in the previous sections, the organization controlling all publishing rights versus the songwriter retaining the publishing rights, are that there are two general types of contracts between songwriters and publishing companies. Those types of contracts are respectively called *assignment* and *licensing*. The type of agreement used depends on the type of arrangement. In a nutshell, the writer either *assigns* the company all publishing rights *in perpetuity*—or until either party is notified in writing with a separation request—or the songwriter transfers all publishing rights on a temporary basis. I recommend the first path, assignment, for a faith-based organization. This is the basic Hillsong Publishing model.

No matter which type of contract, the commitment the publishing company has to the songwriters—who are willing to transfer their ownership of the rights to their work—breaks down into four areas. These areas are the heart and soul of your publishing company.

- Ownership of the copyright
- Income source distribution
- Exploitation commitment
- Duration of the contract

There *must* be a commitment to free-flowing, heartfelt communication between organization leadership and songwriters. Otherwise, mistrust will creep into the room. Legal and relationship management is much less complicated when you write *assignment-only* agreements. If you establish these agreements, then you have responsibility for the four bullet points above.

A *licensing* agreement, by definition, is that the company acts on behalf of a writer as their publisher for a *specified period*. At the end of that period, all rights revert to the author.

If you have a licensing agreement, you most likely won't have ownership of the copyright, and the other three in the list above become responsibilities with caveats and limitations. I will describe the consequences with either type agreement, assignment or licensing, beginning with ownership of the copyright.

OWNERSHIP OF THE COPYRIGHT

Assignment contracts mean that you intend to enter an, often long-term, agreement with a songwriter. This means the contract will award the organization exclusive authority to exercise all publishing rights of the song. The contract will also stipulate that the organization will own the copyright of the song. Remember, only the holder of a registered copyright may enter litigation or infringement settlement negotiations. Fear not, control of the copyright never interferes with credit of the original author.

The copyright is assigned to the publisher for their protection *and* the songwriter's. The publisher will have indisputable legal right to notify authorities about any registration status changes for the songs (for example, performance rights and royalty organizations). Without an assignment of the copyright, publishing companies leave themselves open to legal challenges for these types of status changes, as well as any claims of conflicting transfers or lost revenue. A recorded copyright transfer can provide "constructive notice" and *prima facie* evidence in a court of law, meaning that other parties cannot make claim to the contrary. Although many smaller publishing companies have often skipped this step, *it's a fool's errand to be insufficiently prepared for any possible angle in infringement litigation.*

I want to further emphasize that only the holder of a registered copyright may begin infringement litigation. It is best to be prepared for this eventuality and to go to bat for your songwriters.

This assignment of copyright doesn't happen often with licensing agreements. There are three main reasons to assign the copyright:

1. The person or entity who controls the copyright has the indisputable legal right to notify authorities about registration status changes on the song, as just mentioned.

2. As also mentioned, only the holder of the copyright can instigate litigation on its behalf. The flip side is that the holder of the copyright is responsible for defending against an infringement lawsuit *and* is most likely liable for any damages awarded.

3. The request to transfer the copyright from songwriter to the faith-based music publisher sends a message that the company believes in the songwriter.

With short-term licensing agreements, the publishing company can only control status changes for a specified period and then is required to "undo" all that paperwork at the end of the period.

It's a risk to the company if they sign a licensing agreement with a songwriter *and* transfer the copyright for the reasons of copyright infringement lawsuits—because it's a temporary relationship. All publishing contracts have the writer attest to the originality of their work, but in the worst case, it's still a large amount of money and time spent to go to court to defend a song that is no longer yours …

The faith-based publishing company must also place faith in their songwriters for the sake of maintaining a family or a dedicated-purpose atmosphere. Although it may be advisable to transfer the copyright in a licensing agreement for reason number one above, it can become too risky for organizations to sign unknown songs because of reason number two above.

All of this should be taken to an attorney.

INCOME SOURCE DISTRIBUTION

Here are possible revenue sources for your new company:

- Physical and digital sales of recordings
  - CDs, mp3s, and mp4s

- Digital performance and streaming royalties
- Print and digital sales of sheet music
  - Individual sheet music and folios, non-CCLI

- Mechanical reproduction license fees
  - Others who want to record your song

- Synchronization license fees for film, TV, and other entertainment media
  - For the underlying work
  - Master use licenses for the request of a specific recording

- Grand Rights
  - When your music is used on the drama stage

- Foreign Royalties
  - Royalties and usage fees collected outside your country

- PRO royalties
  - ASCAP, BMI, SESAC, and AllTrack in the US
  - Live performance of the underlying work

- CCLI
  - Church copyright license royalties
  - Church streaming license royalties
  - SongSelect royalties

- Unforeseen collections
- Income from exploitation not on this list, or from technology yet known

Note that for assignment agreements, all the revenue from the above falls naturally along the list. The majority of possible revenue sources above depend on a longer-term relationship to build up the income pipeline for the product. With a licensing agreement, the revenue generated for those income sources stop. There is an end date to the agreement with the songwriter, and the publisher must generate paperwork to sever all income streams. The reason is that when there is an end date, the relationship is over and all publishing rights revert to the songwriter. Of course, every situation is negotiable.

EXPLOITATION COMMITMENT

With an assignment agreement, you'll describe the organization's commitment to the songwriter and identify all the mutual goals for the symbiotic relationship: The common goal of becoming the best songwriter possible to deliver the best quality songs possible to the church. But the organization's commitment is to also build up the reputation of the writer and to do everything possible to make their works available.

On the other hand, if the organization enters a licensing agreement, there may be a common goal of delivering the best songs to the church, but it would be the responsibility of the songwriter to find any future uses for their songs or to write contracts for them when this term expires. The songwriter would be on their own to manage their catalog of songs, unless there was a separate and future administration agreement.

DURATION OF THE CONTRACT

If an assignment agreement is used, the usual contract obligation for both parties is for the life of the copyright, that is, life of the author plus 70 years. *In perpetuity* is common language, meaning forever until either party wants to cancel in writing. This can give a sense of continuity for rights management and assurance there will always be an advocate for the song.

With licensing agreements, there is a guarantee the agreement will have an end date. This will lead to uncertainty and more administration work to revert the rights to the songwriter. There may be apprehension that the organization will fail to change ownership information for songs which will impact royalty payout and the required organizational accounting adjustments.

OTHER COMMITMENTS

I've covered the Big Four obligations of the publishing company to the songwriter. Here are a few brief obligations that are just as important.

MASTER RECORDING TRANSFER

Since your organization will publish sound recordings and own the master, you should specify the desired timeline, if any, for transferring the ownership of the master to the author. In the event the songwriter wanted the master recording ownership to revert to them at the end of the contract period, they would be responsible for all recording costs and buy-out cost of the master.

The master recording is usually owned by the creator of the recording. This gives them the opportunity to issue master licenses for those who wish to use the recording. In addition, there are sync licenses issued for the underlying use of the composition. Both of these income streams will be lost to the organization. The songwriter will recover these rights, which is good. But they wouldn't have to pay any money at all if they didn't request owning the masters for that period of time.

SONGS

Decide if all songs from the writer or only select ones are to be assigned to you as the publisher. Examples: maybe you decide that the only songs you'll sign from the writer will be by invitation. Or you could decide that all songs are works made for hire if you employ the songwriter.

TERMINATION

You need to specify the conditions and methods when a writer or you request to terminate any contract.

TERRITORY

The contract with the writer needs to specify your level of commitment of coverage to your country of origin or to the world.

Again, seek professional legal advice for all the above.

TIPS FOR A FAITH-BASED PUBLISHER

- *Publishing companies should join all PROs:* ASCAP, BMI, SESAC and AllTrack in the US so you will be prepared to sign any writer. Songwriters are free to join any PRO, but only one.
- *The songwriter and the publisher both need to register at Sound Exchange* in the US for digital performance royalties. You should be aware that the Music Modernization Act of 2018, https://

en.wikipedia.org/wiki/Music_Modernization_ Act, in the US has declared a new digital royalty payout scheme. See the section *Worship songwriter action list: prepare and register now for royalty payments* under *PROs and performance royalties* earlier in this chapter to see the action plan to register your songs.

- *Sign up as a music rights holder at CCLI*, whether as a publishing company or as an individual. They always ask the percentage of ownership question during any song upload session. You can assign exact percentages to other rights owners who are members or indicate that your share is 100%.

- *If the songwriting organization collects all CCLI royalties for the writers*, the organization will claim 100% and then distribute whatever is agreed upon to the writers.

- *Spell out the exact methods you intend to collect and distribute fees and royalties*, and the times and methods you will account to the writers.

- *If your leadership team decides to sign both types of writing contracts* (assignment and licensing), write out a complete plan, including a ledger with the pros and cons so you know all consequences. Maybe you and your leadership team will be creative. No rules.

  - Having the two types of writer contracts going, which is what mainstream publishers do, places the emphasis of being in business on taking in the most revenue possible. Consider the emphasis of this model—*The Proverbs 27:17 Model*—of being in business for seeking the kingdom of God first, money second!

- o Like I've said, there's nothing wrong with making money, but I believe it would be too divisive to write both types of contracts. It could cause disharmony and become a distraction.
- o There could be unforeseen consequences about offering both types of contracts. Let this decision come from *your* imagination.

PUBLISHING COMPANY SUMMARY

Your new publishing company is unique because its primary purpose is of the heart; the organization seeks to honor God in the local community first and all other opportunities second. If your songwriting organization is called to publish and make the songs known to the wider world, you now have a recipe to accomplish work in local song theology and expanding that ideology to a larger audience.

To amplify what was written earlier: I recommend that you seek the same model as Hillsong Publishing and offer assignment contracts with the writers, and not licensing. At the risk of confusion, it's important you understand both types.

You might think going to these extremes is overkill. In some cases, you might be right. But if you're not legally and organizationally prepared if or when a larger music company comes along and wants to purchase yours, you will not be getting yourself, your family, or your songwriters their best deal. Or if, God forbid, someone wished to take you to court for infringement, you could lose it all.

It's all for the glory of God, but the greediness of man doesn't care about your praise of him.

NEXT STEPS

I pray that *The 5 Steps to Get Your Songs Heard* changes your life. The idea behind it has changed mine. If you're willing, please join me in getting this idea out to songwriters, musicians, worship leaders, sound technicians, and administration support people in your church. Lend them your copy of this book or point them to https://getyoursongsheard.com or https://stephenrobertcass.com/books.

Please leave an honest review of each of my books which you will find at my Amazon author page, http://amazon.com/authors/stephenrobertcass

If you would like to contact like-minded songwriters in your area to build relationships and to take the next step in the Small-Church Local Song Theology Revolution, enter your name and email address at https://songs4god.net/like-minded-songwriters (protected page: password is SCLSTR).

As you enter your name, I will place it on a list and post that link on the same page. The list will have names and email addresses segmented into states or countries. Plan to connect with other songwriters and co-write and talk about creating a songwriting organization.

What's next? You'll find the expanded version of this idea and many more details about it in my book *Fishing in Church*. Also available are other books and e-books describing the individual tools and topics: *The Proverbs 27.17 Lyric Formula, The Proverbs 27.17 Melody Shape Tool, The Proverbs 27.17 Song Critique Method, Worship Songs and the Law: How Churches Stay Legal and Songwriters Get Paid*, and *The Christian Songwriter's Guide to Royalties* at my website or wherever you like to find books.

I will also be available to come to your church, songwriting meetings, conferences, or any event to tell you more about *The 5 Steps to Get Your Songs Heard* and *Fishing in Church*. Please see https://stephenrobertcass.com/speaking.

If you are a songwriter called by God, be convinced that learning and applying the ways of congregational songwriting will fulfill your dream of getting your songs heard while fulfilling God's plan for your life. You need to define that plan. My hope is that you have found that plan in these pages. It's not a plan of pie-in-the-sky promises of fame and fortune, it's more a guarantee you can't go wrong aligning your ministry with Jesus's ministry for his church on Earth.

Become an agent for the Father in his effort to save the world through his Son, Jesus. Join the Great Commission and learn how you can go forth and make disciples through the gift God has given you.

Join me and learn the unique pathway of *congregational* songwriting. There is no such training available anywhere. The music industry has wonderful staff songwriters, such as Grammy-nominated, Dove Award-winning songwriter Krissy Nordhoff (*Your Great Name*, recorded by Natalie Grant, for example). Krissy has her own songwriting outreach ministry at https://krissynordhoff.com. She and

I know that the pathway to writing professional, heartfelt, *local theology* worship songs lies with our individual efforts to build and encourage the songwriters of local church communities. The major record companies do not share these goals. We rise to the challenge of encouraging songwriters around the world to write Holy Spirit-filled songs that mean everything to local communities.

LOCAL SONG THEOLOGY: SEEK FIRST THE KINGDOM

This is how we prayerfully accomplish *local song theology*: we can capture and characterize the strengths of people in our communities as we witness God at work in their lives. We can write or co-write spiritual songs about what we witness, songs that move our own hearts to worship because we see the love of God at work. The goal is to make Jesus famous by serving our local communities with our songs.

Matthew 6:33 is the clarion call for Christ followers to seek the kingdom of God and his righteousness as our first priority. We set our minds on it; we resolve to do it, not for personal gain, but to bring him glory.

> *But seek first his kingdom and his righteousness,*
> *and all these things will be given to you as well.*

Matthew chapters 5, 6, and 7 record the teachings of Jesus on the Mount of Olives. In chapter 5 he spoke to those who were poor in spirit, he called them blessed. He said, "Blessed are the poor in spirit, for theirs is the kingdom of God." And he talked about people who were marginalized, suppressed, poor, those who showed mercy, those who would bring peace, and those who were persecuted for the sake of righteousness. He called them blessed, too. Our songs can capture and characterize people in our own communities who are blessed in similar circumstances, and we can encourage them and our local congregations to hang in there, to trust Jesus and to be faithful.

Jesus also said that we should seek his righteousness. "Righteousness" as written here in the original Greek is *dikaiosuné,* which referred to a characteristic of God, or human action in the original Hebrew language, *tsadaq:* to be or to make right in a moral sense. Jesus was clearly referring to how it is God's desire to administer his righteousness to people *by people.* By writing and sharing our congregational songs of worship we become the people God uses to administer his righteousness, bringing people into the presence of our Lord in worship, teaching them how to live victoriously in their circumstances.

We are all instruments in bringing God's sense of justice to the world, and it is my prayer that we songwriters do our part.

Jesus said to let our light shine before others that they may see our good deeds (Matthew 5:14–16); that we should give to the poor in silence rather than boasting (Matthew 6:2–4); that we should not labor and spin in vain about the things we need (Matthew 6:30–43); and that we should not judge people (Matthew 7:1–5). Rather, we should ask, seek, and knock on the door of opportunities as we find they align with God's desire for us to live righteously. He tells us when we seek the face of God first, our perspectives about "things" in our life change. As we concentrate on *tsdadaq,* we honor God by making his Son famous and pointing others to his kingdom plan.

How marvelous is the call of Jesus on my heart! May we all seek to serve our communities with the clear call of Jesus to act. God calls songwriters to be in touch with people and to help tell their stories of struggles and victories and lead them to the foot of the cross. This will strengthen us all and give genuine life and heart to our songs. Our songs certainly are not on par with the kingdom of God. But they do trumpet the kingdom of God, and we can be his instrument.

AN INSPIRATIONAL CALL TO ACTION

This is not about making money. If or when money comes, so be it. Use it to perpetuate the organization. There's nothing wrong with creating a business model that makes money. Build it remembering these primary goals:

- Educate and nurture solid and sought-after songwriters.
- Write and deliver songs on how God is moving in your community.
- Record and market the best songs to the wider world.

This idea goes well beyond what an average songwriting organization might do because of the dedication to fishing in church and local song theology. There will be more than workshops, exercises, and open mic nights. The central design is to raise the skills of the songwriter. The songwriting organization will publish, promote, record, and release songs that show our dedication to quality and searching through the grass roots.

If you "start small" with two or three writers, be encouraged by the Savior in Matthew 18:20: *"Where two or three gather in my name, there I am with them."* If you are a new songwriter, or accept the challenge of creating this new organization, don't let the talk of publishing, promoting, recording, and releasing songs stop you or intimidate you. You can work up to these things.

Take on the serious responsibility to make your dreams come true. No matter your goals, whether to start writing or to become a better writer, or whether to start a songwriting community or to get your songs recorded, here is a tried-and-true approach that I pray inspires you. I invite you to plug in your own statement for:

- My problem statements.
- My objectives.
- My key results.
- How to measure my key results.

My problem statements:

I am driven by God to write songs. No one wants to listen to my songs. What do I do?
Or
I am driven by God to write songs. I want to learn to write or to get better at writing them. How can I achieve this?
Or
I am ready to create a faith-based songwriting organization. How do I go about that?

Objectives are aspirational goals. They are the Big Picture. They are the solution to your problem statements.

My objective:

Get my songs heard by learning the skills of the congregational songwriter.

Why?

1. So that I can share skilled songs with my church or other songwriters.
2. I will be able to feel like I am accomplishing my call from God.
3. I can finally realize that I am taking part in the kingdom work of God.
4. So that the Gospel of Jesus Christ is heard clearly in churches.
5. Because I can become a sought-after songwriter to co-write songs.
6. So that I am seen as a skilled songwriter and an asset to worship leaders in my community.
7. I can become an expert and show others the skills of congregational songwriting.

By spending the time to ask yourself *why*, you discover the deep meaning of what motivates you. This is important so you might write deeper objectives and make plans to pursue the right courses of action.

Key Results are measurable steps to achieve your objective. Yours will vary from mine. They are not individual tasks or tactics. Those will come in the next steps after listing the KRs. The following KRs are only examples.

My key results:

1. Write 10 songs and present them to the songwriting community song critique forum.
2. Get 15 songs recorded and uploaded to Spotify so we can create a playlist to send out to local worship leaders.
3. Upload 20 song lyrics to CCLI so they are available to 250,000 churches around the world.

How should you measure your progress and why? When you create specific and measurable tasks that include a due date, your projects will progress. The examples are given below. These are your tactics or tasks.

How to measure my key results (examples only):

1. (example for KR 1) Set aside 2 hours per day for songwriting, with a deadline of March 1 for those 10 songs.
2. (example for KR 2) Prepare the song files for 2 songs or more each day to prepare musicians for the recording session deadline of March 1.
3. (example for KR 3) Gather all necessary lyric files for a March 1 upload session at CCLI's rights holder song portal.

Now imagine how amplified your writing, recording, and marketing efforts will be when you tackle this challenge of objectives and key results as an entire songwriting organization. For as iron sharpens iron, we most definitely sharpen each other.

"Two are better than one, because they have
a good return for their labor: If either of
them falls down, one can help the other up."
(Ecclesiastes 4:9–10 NIV)

You don't even have to start this organization. Use the dedicated congregational songwriting education in this book and in *Fishing in Church* to sharpen your saw, and maybe you can interest others who would lean in that direction and show them the organization plans in this book.

Jesus taught the disciples that becoming fishers of people is a team sport. That's where it starts. Though there's not much written about these men, their families and their entourage, I can imagine they reached out to other fishermen and like-minded people for support, as well as leaning on each other. They eventually realized that using whatever talents they had and depending on the surrounding people to magnify their efforts was the lesson that Jesus taught them. That's the meaning of the loaves and fishes; that God will multiply their efforts when they make good with what they have and as they're able to add faith. Faith that God will always be with them when they align their purposes with his.

As songwriters, we learn how to fish with songwriting tools and learn how to better our craft. There's no stronger craft tool than banding together with like-minded songwriters that want to reach hearts for God. Gather so we can sharpen each other. That's the very best of strategies.

Let faith fill the void where the fear of being alone *was* in your heart.

This new idea for a songwriting community differs from any other organization because it flows from the central and common hunger to get our songs heard and feed our local communities. We learn congregational lyric and melody writing to magnify our desire to help each other learn, grow, and succeed. Our victories become a part of our contribution to help spread the Good News.

Be a part of it and become a change-agent for Christ with your songs.

> *"I know what it is to be in need, and I know what it is to have plenty. I have learned the secret of being content in any and every situation, whether well fed or hungry, whether living in plenty or in want. I can do all this through him who gives me strength."*
>
> Philippians 4:12–13

ABOUT THE AUTHOR

Stephen Robert Cass is a hack golfer who aims for high mediocrity. Because of his lofty goals on the course, he may one day enter charity tournaments so he can donate his time and talents. When not swinging for the fences, he's known for:

- ❑ 50+ years as a worship musician and team member,
- ❑ 14 years as a worship leader,
- ❑ 27 years as a published Christian songwriter,
- ❑ 15 album projects, whether solo, produced or musician credits,
- ❑ 70+ worship song titles found at CCLI under the Solid Walnut Music catalog and Stephen Robert Cass.

Solid Walnut Music has given away original music CDs to Christian radio stations all over the world: the US, Canada, Mexico, Australia, England, Ireland, Russia, Ethiopia, Bulgaria, Italy, South Africa, South Korea, and Israel.

Go to https://getyoursongsheard.com, so your friends can receive this book plus bonuses.

Visit https://amazon.com/author/stephenrobertcass to see all major books and e-book releases.

See https://stephenrobertcass.com for all other e-book releases, the press kit, and speaking engagements.

Swing by https://songs4god.net for songwriting blogs and other information about Steve.

Contact steve@songs4god.net.